The Crocodile

Look for these and other books in the
Lucent Endangered Animals and Habitats Series:

The Amazon Rain Forest
The Bald Eagle
Bats
The Bear
Birds of Prey
The Cheetah
The Condor
Coral Reefs
Dolphins and Porpoises
The Elephant
The Giant Panda
The Gorilla
The Jaguar
The Manatee
The Oceans
The Orangutan
The Rhinoceros
Seals and Sea Lions
The Shark
The Tiger
The Whale
The Wolf

Other related titles in the Lucent Overview Series:

Endangered Species
Energy Alternatives
Environmental Groups
Garbage
Hazardous Waste
Oil Spills
Ozone
Population
Saving the American Wilderness
Zoos

THE CROCODILE

BY KARYN FOLLIS CHEATHAM

Endangered Animals & Habitats

LUCENT BOOKS, INC.
SAN DIEGO, CALIFORNIA

LUCENT Overview Series

Cover Photo: Saltwater crocodile, Australia.

Library of Congress Cataloging-in-Publication Data

Cheatham, K. Follis (Karyn Follis), 1943–
The Crocodile / by Karyn Follis Cheatham.
p. cm. — (Endangered animals & habitats)
Includes bibliographical references and index (p.).
Summary: Discusses the crocodiles of the world, the threats to their existence such as hunting and habitat loss and the efforts to save and protect them including captive breeding, catch-and-release programs and the use of parks and reserves.
ISBN 1-56006-833-7 (hardback : alk. paper)
1. Crocodiles—Juvenile literature. 2. Endangered species—Juvenile literature. [1. Crocodiles. 2. Endangered species.] I. Title. II. Series.
QL666.C925 C477 2001
597.98'2—dc21

00-011271

P.O. Box 289011, San Diego, CA 92198-9011
Printed in the U.S.A.

Contents

Introduction

CROCODILES ARE THE largest reptiles on earth and the last direct link with the dinosaurs. Unlike their notorious relatives, though, they have managed to survive. Scientists are still investigating how these animals managed to do so, but the fact remains that crocodiles have endured ice ages, climate changes and geological movements of continents. These situations caused other animals to evolve into different species or to die out, but the crocodile has remained virtually the same.

In recent times, however, this ancient creature has suffered some serious problems. During the 1970s crocodiles were on the verge of extinction because they were overhunted for their skins. Changes in international hunting laws decreased that severe threat, however, and today most populations have made a dramatic comeback. But even with these laws in place, many of the world's fourteen species of crocodiles are still considered endangered.

In calling for crocodile protection, herpetologists (people who study reptiles and amphibians) point out that crocodiles are a keystone species. That means they are vital to the maintenance of the wetlands in which they live. As the largest predators in their ecosystem, crocodiles help maintain the balance among other animals, fish, and plants. In Africa, for instance, they eat dead hippopotamuses and other creatures that, if left to rot, would pollute the riverbanks. The waste that crocodiles produce has a positive effect on the nutrients in the soil, aiding the growth of trees and other plants. The holes crocodiles make while nesting and burrowing eventually fill with water; these little oases become vital to other birds and small mammals during times of drought. Even the depressions and trails left in the mud by their heavy tails become vital sources of water where small fish and amphibians can live. Crocodiles, therefore, are a vital aid to the maintenance of their ecosystems. Without crocodiles, some habitats would be devastated by drought and others would be overrun with certain types of fish and mammals, whose increased numbers eventually could not be supported.

Efforts to preserve crocodiles and their habitats receive increased attention every day, but it is often difficult to convince people that the animals should be saved. When most people look at a crocodile, with its stubby legs and toothy grin, they find it hard to think the animal might

Crocodiles are the largest reptiles on earth.

have more value than its scaly skin. Furthermore, movies and television programs often show crocodiles as fearsome predators that attack other animals—and people—which makes it difficult to think that crocodiles need to be saved from anything.

But researchers agree that crocodiles and the environments they inhabit are some of the most at-risk fauna and flora in the world. In the twenty-first century, if crocodiles are to continue their return from near extinction, important decisions about conservation methods for the animal and

Crocodiles were almost hunted to extinction because of the demand for their skins.

The First True Crocodile

Deinosuchus (pronounced *dy-no-su-chess*) rugosus is considered by many herpetologists to be the first true crocodile, and a skull of the animal, found in the Rio Grande area of the United States, is more than six feet long. Researchers estimate that Deinosuchus, also called the terrible crocodile, was nearly fifty feet long and weighed about six tons. Deinosuchus bones have been found in the Carolinas, Georgia, Alabama, Montana, and the southwestern United States.

its environment are necessary. Also important is an improvement in the way most people think about crocodiles. Herpetologists and conservationists are exploring many ways to accomplish all of this. They hope they will succeed and that their success will result in the ultimate survival for this very adaptable creature.

1

The Specialized Reptile

CROCODILES HAVE ALWAYS been quite successful at adjusting to changes in their environments. They can live comfortably in water or on land, and they are known for their ability to withstand incredible injuries, long periods of drought, and lack of food. This adaptability is one of the major reasons they have lasted for so many millions of years.

Crocodiles bear the name of the scientific order in which they are classified: Crocodilia. In the three Crocodilia subfamilies are listed twenty-three species. Crocodiles make up the largest subfamily, with fourteen different species. Alligators and caimans, close cousins of the crocodile, make up the second subfamily; the gharial (with only one species) comprises the third. Crocodiles, unlike the other two subfamilies, are unique because they can be found in more regions of the world than any other crocodilian.

Crocodiles are reptiles

All crocodilians are reptiles. Reptiles are the first class of animals with a vertebrae—that is, a backbone—to live on land and have their young develop in hard-shelled eggs. Crocodiles and other reptiles breathe through lungs rather than through temporary or permanent gills the way tadpoles and fish do. Because of these features, reptiles are better adapted for life on dry land than the amphibians from which they descended.

Crocodiles have scales that cover their bodies. These scales are often referred to as an exoskeleton, or outside skeleton. This durable exoskeleton covers the back of the head, tail, sides, and legs of crocodiles, including their feet. The scales grow in a pattern on the animals' bodies and provide excellent protection from heavy objects they might encounter while swimming or maneuvering on land.

As with all reptiles, crocodiles are also poikilothermic, or cold-blooded, animals. This means their body temperature is dependent on the temperature of their environment. When the surrounding temperature increases or decreases, the animals' body temperature also increases or decreases. Since crocodiles' nonoverlapping scales do not offer much insulation, the animals depend on the warmth of the sun to raise their body temperatures high enough for them to become mobile and for their digestive and respiratory system

Crocodiles can live in water or on land, and they adapt easily to changes in the environment.

About Reptiles

Today more than six thousand species of reptiles exist—but that is quite a few less than existed 175 million years ago, when reptiles were the most successful creatures on the earth. The first reptile was the hylonomus, a large, lizardlike creature, and from that animal developed small creatures such as geckos and other lizards as well as the massive dinosaurs—the largest animals ever. Sixteen orders of reptiles once existed, but now there are only four: squamates (which make up 90 percent of the reptile class), tuataras, turtles, and crocodilians.

to function without stress. This need limits the type of habitats in which crocodiles may live. For instance, they have never been found over a 3,260-foot elevation, where nighttime temperatures can drop below forty degrees.

To adjust their body temperature, many crocodile species bask in sunshine to get warm. If they become too warm, they can open their large mouths and the evaporation of moisture from their mouths will lower their body temperature. If the weather becomes too hot, they can crawl under shrubbery or return to the water. Many crocodiles remain burrowed in mud or stay in water during the hot daylight hours; they become more active at night, when the temperature on land is more comfortable for them.

Being cold blooded has many benefits. First of all, when poikilothermic creatures do not have adequate warmth around them, their body systems slow down while they wait for the environmental temperature to change, thus lessening the needs of their circulatory and respiratory systems. Also, crocodiles do not have to create energy to stay warm, meaning they can survive for long periods without much food. In fact, an adult crocodile, although known to be an aggressive predator, could live with only one full meal a year.

Mammalian traits

Crocodiles are the largest and most advanced of all reptiles alive today. Although reptiles are the predecessors of birds and mammals and much of their makeup mirrors what can be found in these later developed animals, crocodiles are more similar to mammals than other reptiles are. For example, their eyes, which are set close together on the top of their heads, give them binocular vision—meaning what is seen from each eye intersects to provide accurate depth perception. This is very important when they are hunting. Even underwater, crocodiles can determine the exact distance between themselves and their prey.

Crocodiles also have a bony palate that separates their mouths from their nostrils. With their nostrils out of water,

Even though crocodiles are reptiles, they possess many mammalian traits, including eyes that are close together on top of their heads.

Crocodiles are the only reptiles that can move either by walking (as seen here) or by sliding along on their bellies like lizards.

they can breathe even when their mouths are filled with water. Their mouths are also constructed with a palatal valve at the back that prevents water from going into their throats. This allows crocodiles to open their mouths underwater to catch fish. As with humans and other mammals, water will not go down their throat until they swallow.

Further, crocodiles and their relatives are the only order of reptiles that can move with their bodies either on or above the ground. On land, crocodiles can scramble along like lizards, moving one short leg at a time with their bellies on the ground. But they can also walk with their bodies off the ground. When crocodiles walk, their gait looks quite similar to that of four-legged mammals.

The brains of crocodiles are also more advanced than those of other reptiles. They have a true cerebral cortex, which allows them to exhibit learned behaviors as opposed to the mostly instinctive behaviors of other reptiles. Crocodiles learn quickly and can adjust to many changes in their environment. According to James Perran Ross, a leading crocodilian researcher at the Florida Museum of Natural History, "[Crocodiles] particularly learn to avoid dangerous situations. For research purposes, we find that we often have to change capture techniques, because it's very hard to catch them with the same trick twice."[1] This ability to learn may explain how they have adapted so well to all of the changes in their long history.

Where crocodiles live

Because they are cold blooded, crocodiles can exist only in equatorial and temperate regions of the world. They can

An Ancient Reverence

In ancient Egypt numerous crocodiles lived in the Nile River and its tributaries. The creature's ability to live both on land and in water made it special, and the Egyptian god Sobek, who was depicted as a man with a crocodile head, was believed to bring fertility from the Nile waters. At that time, Sobek represented the power of the pharaohs. Remnants of temples built for him remain today, and in the city of Arsinoe (which the Greeks called Crocodilopolis), hundreds of crocodiles were adorned with jewels and were kept in large garden pools. The sacred crocodiles were also killed, and their mummified bodies have been found in tombs and pyramids throughout North Africa.

An Egyptian temple relief sculpture of Sobek, a crocodile-headed god.

be found in warm lowland marshes and lagoons, along coastlines and rivers of five different continents, and on tropical islands. These regions are called tropical wetlands. They include jungles; the remote rivers and rain forests of South and Central America, Africa, and India; swamplands in Australia; and many equatorial archipelagos, such as New Guinea, the Philippines, and Madagascar. Crocodiles are the largest land-based predator to live in so many parts of the world.

Most crocodile habitats are heavy with vegetation and tall trees, and a large number of them are part of tropical rain forests, which cover more than 4 million square miles of the wettest land in the world. These rain forests contain 90 percent of the world's animals and plant species, including almost every known crocodilian.

Crocodiles are also found in the muddy, sheltered seashores of the equator's mangrove swamps. Although some mangrove swamps grow in temperate regions, such as the south coast of Florida and the northern part of the Indian Ocean, most are on tropical coasts throughout Asia, India,

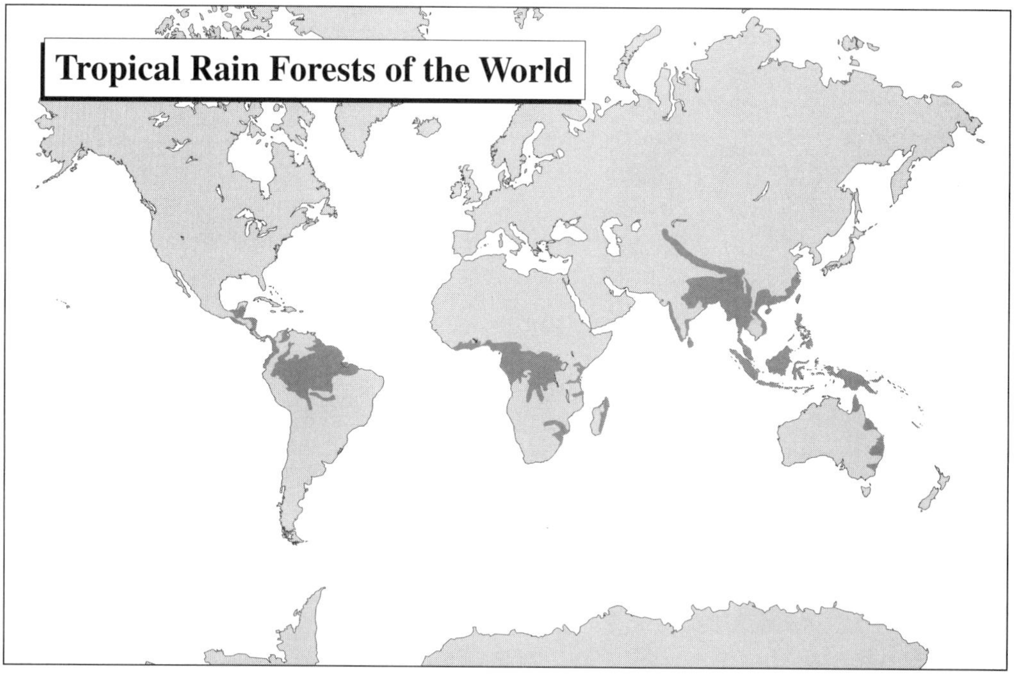

Tropical Rain Forests of the World

Africa, and South America. Mangrove trees, which make up most of the vegetation in the swamps, are evergreens that have adapted to the salty conditions of coastlines, where they are flooded twice a day by seawater. Crocodiles have also adapted to these conditions, mostly because of a gland in their mouths that collects salt from brackish waters; the animals can then expel the salt when they are on land.

Although crocodiles generally make their homes in these areas, they can swim far out in the ocean. Estuarine crocodiles, for example, have been seen more than two hundred miles out to sea, and the American crocodile has been reported to swim several hundreds of ocean miles to reach islands.

Physical characteristics

Crocodiles live long lives. In fact, with a life span of seventy to one hundred years, crocodiles are one of the longest-living creatures on the earth. The largest species, the estuarine crocodile, can grow to twenty-three feet in length and weigh more than a ton; in contrast, the dwarf crocodile can be as small as four feet in length and weigh less than eight hundred pounds.

Each crocodile species grows in proportion to its diet and environment. Thus, a big crocodile that has lived in a good, warm environment with abundant food may be a whole decade younger than a smaller crocodile of the same species that lives in less favorable conditions. Despite these variations in size, though, crocodiles never stop growing. Because of this, scientists can examine a dead crocodile and determine its exact age; cross-sections of its bones will have growth rings, just like a tree.

Crocodiles' bodies are built so that it is easy for them to get around in their lush tropical habitats. Low to the ground, their bodies are wide and flat. Their heads protrude horizontally in front of their bodies, and they have long snouts that help them push through dense foliage. Their eyes and nostrils are located on the top of their skull. Their tail drags behind them when they crawl; when they walk with their body off the ground, however, their tail,

The Differences Between Crocodiles and Alligators

Crocodiles and alligators are both members of the order Crocodilia, but they have unique characteristics that make it easy to distinguish one from the other. According to the website of the American Museum of Natural History, there are several ways to tell the animals apart.

> Look at the lower front teeth. On both sides of the lower jaw of crocodiles, the fourth tooth from the front of the snout is visible when the animal's mouth is closed. When an alligator's mouth is closed, you can't see any of its lower teeth. Alligators have . . . broad snouts. Crocodiles have . . . narrow snouts. Alligators' coloring is darker than that of crocodiles. If you hear one of these big reptiles bellowing, it's an alligator. Crocodiles don't bellow and are far less vocal in general.

The physiology of the two orders is also different. For instance, alligators can live only in freshwater because they do not have a gland in their mouth to expel salt, and they can tolerate colder temperatures than crocodiles, allowing them to live in what are called temperate regions, like the southern marshes of the United States. Crocodiles must have warmer, tropical temperatures.

At first glance, crocodiles and alligators (pictured) may appear alike, but there are distinct differences.

which is more than one-third of their body length, swings in a rhythmic S movement. Their feet are very broad and have five toes on the front and four partially webbed toes on the back.

Although crocodiles can move swiftly on land, they maneuver best when in the water.

At first appearance their short legs do not seem very strong, but that is a misconception. In fact, many crocodiles have very strong legs and can move quite swiftly on land. Nile crocodiles, for instance, have been known to reach short bursts of speed of up to twenty-nine miles per hour. Crocodiles can also leap forward up to three feet and jump into the air as high as five feet, depending on the species.

Moving in the water, though, is what crocodiles do best. Crocodiles swim with their long bodies just below the waterline. They usually cruise with their legs up against their bodies while their high nostrils and eyes protrude above the surface, allowing them to breathe and see where they are going. Their oarlike tails also move in the same S motion as when they walk on land, and this back-and-forth movement propels them through the water. The tail acts as both a rudder and a motor, and it can send them in short bursts at speeds of up to fifteen miles per hour. They can quickly change speed and direction as well, and their webbed back feet help them launch their heads and bodies out of the water in a "tail walk" similar to dolphins.

Other physical features enable crocodiles to easily negotiate through their watery habitats. When crocodiles are in water, they can float their bodies on top of the water, for example, or take more air into their lungs and sink below the surface. Special flaps cover their ears to prevent water from entering their elongated ear canals. They also have a third transparent eyelid, called a nictitating membrane, which closes over the eyes for protection from debris when underwater. A fluid released by a gland behind this membrane also acts to clean the eyes and prevent them from drying out when the animal is out of the water.

How crocodiles develop

Crocodiles, like all reptiles, hatch from eggs. Several months in advance of laying their eggs, females build nests in sheltered areas near the freshwater where they will raise their young. Some species create mounds several feet deep on banks near the water, and others dig deep holes under vegetation or in sandbars.

Mating usually takes place once each year in the springtime or before the region's rainy season. In Africa, this is often in October; in the Indo-Pacific region, it would be in May. Before mating, crocodiles court each other by making loud noises and nuzzling together.

After mating, the female lays between twelve and eighty (depending on the species) tough-shelled eggs in the nest and then covers them with mud and vegetation. Although it varies by species, the nest area ranges in size from two to five feet in width, and the heaps of vegetation used for mound nesting are usually more than a foot high. This is important protection for the eggs. Since crocodiles do not incubate their eggs by sitting on them, the nest must maintain the eggs at temperatures of eighty to ninety-five degrees Fahrenheit. Temperatures lower or higher than this will destroy the embryos.

This female crocodile prepares to lay eggs by digging a hole for a nest with her snout.

It can take up to three months for a crocodile to form completely inside the egg, a time period that is hazardous to the baby. In the countries of southern Asia and regions of Australia, mongooses and monitor lizards very often dig open nests and eat several eggs during these months. Once nests are exposed, birds then peck open the eggs and feed; other lizards and mammals can also consume eggs. The same occurs in Africa and the Americas, where raccoons, monkeys, and other primates scout river and stream banks for crocodile nests to rob. Because of this, only 1 percent of all crocodile eggs laid actually hatch.

Hatching

Part of a crocodile embryo's development includes a small protrusion at the center of its upper jaw, called an egg tooth. It is not really a tooth, however, and it disappears

Many herpetologists call baby crocodiles croakers because of the sounds they make as they hatch.

within a week after the crocodile has hatched. This hornlike piece of skin is tough enough to cut through the inner membrane of the egg, allowing the crocodile to push on the shell to crack it open. Even with the egg tooth, though, some crocodiles are unable to break out of the thick-shelled egg or dig out of the mud nest, which usually has become dried and very hard. Often just their noses will poke through the egg shells, which is enough for them to breathe or make sounds.

Sometimes these problems are avoided because the parents instinctively stay near the nest. This gives the babies a higher hatching rate. Since the adults are close to the nest, they usually hear the sounds of the hatching crocodiles. All of the developed eggs hatch at the same time, and the female digs out the noisy eggs. The sound is so distinctive that many herpetologists call these babies "croakers."

If the baby cannot break through the shell on its own, the mother must gently crack open the egg so the baby is able to hatch. When a parent is not present and the baby cannot crack the shell, it will suffocate inside the egg.

Young crocodiles

The small creatures that emerge from the eggs are tiny replicas of their parents. They measure six to twelve inches long, depending on the species, and have teeth, scaly skin, and big eyes and nostrils.

Once the crocodiles have hatched, their mother must get them to water so they can feed. This often means carrying them in her mouth to get them over rough terrain or through thickets. Mothers of some species, the Nile crocodile in particular, sometimes flip each baby into the air with their noses, catch them in their mouths, and take the youngsters to freshwater.

Freshwater is very important. Although the hatchlings look just like their parents, they lack the special mouth

Mother crocodiles carry their young to freshwater after the babies hatch.

gland to collect salt from brackish water. It will take several years for that gland to develop, and until it does, the babies have to live in freshwater.

Staying safe

The adult must now stay with the young creatures for several months because small crocodiles can become meals for other carnivores. The same animals that eat crocodile eggs also eat baby crocodiles. In the swamps of Cuba, for instance, baby Cuban crocodiles are eaten by their much larger caiman (a type of alligator) cousins. As a result, in all of the crocodile habitats around the world, only a few hatchlings ever reach maturity.

Often adults move through the forests and swamps carrying the youngsters on their backs. This mode of transportation protects the little ones from being eaten by turtles or water snakes, and it allows them to feed on insects that fly overhead. As crocodiles grow larger, they are less likely to be eaten by other animals. Crocodiles grow an average of eight to ten inches each year during the first five years. And if young crocodiles survive six to ten years, they will be big enough to fight off predators themselves and mature enough to start families of their own.

What and how crocodiles eat

Baby crocodiles, just like adults, are carnivores. They eat fish, insects, tadpoles, crustaceans (such as shrimp and crabs) turtles, lizards, and frogs. They also eat birds and mammals. When fresh food is not available, they will eat carrion. Up to 60 percent of what crocodiles eat is converted to fat and is stored in their tails and bodies. This is another reason they can go so long between meals.

To capture their meals, crocodiles use their sixty sharp, cone-shaped teeth. These teeth are uniform in construction and are constantly replaced as the animal grows. A crocodile might have as many as three thousand teeth in its long lifetime.

Although they have teeth, crocodiles cannot chew. Chewing requires a jaw to move from side to side, but

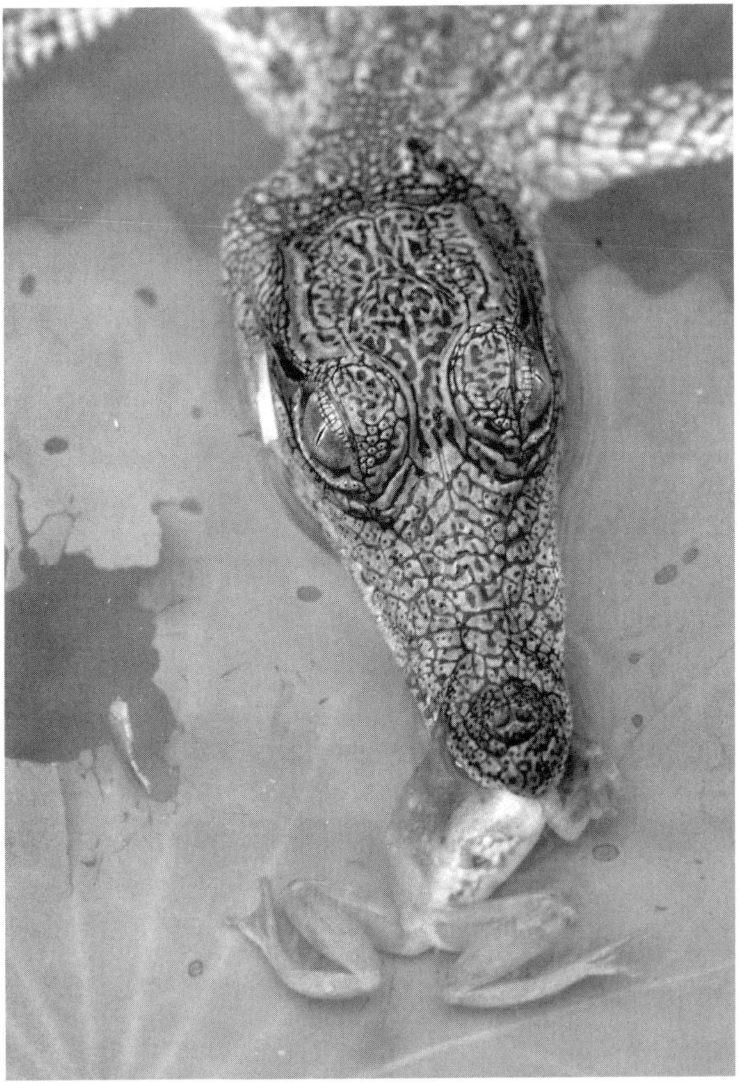

Crocodiles do not chew their food. Instead, they use their teeth to catch a meal and tear it into pieces small enough to swallow.

crocodiles' powerful jaws only move up and down, opening and closing. Because of this, crocodiles must swallow their food whole. Most fish, insects, and crustaceans are easy for them to handle, but when they catch large prey, their teeth impale the creature and they then must yank and tear off hunks small enough to swallow.

Once the food is swallowed, crocodiles' powerful digestive systems take over. The digestive system is so acidic that it dissolves even the shells of crabs and turtles. Crocodiles also have a gizzard to help break down food, and they often swallow stones for the same purpose.

Estivation

Many of the warm wetlands where crocodiles live have hot seasons, during which the ponds and streams dry up and no rain falls. Crocodiles and other cold-blooded animals will protect themselves from these droughts by going into a long sleep, called estivation. Estivation differs from hibernation in that it is triggered by hot weather and not by the cold.

To estivate, crocodiles dig into the mud. They must create a hole large enough for their bodies but small enough to

After swallowing a meal, a crocodile's extremely acidic digestive system goes to work to break down the food.

The Crocodile: Always the Survivor

An article from *Science* magazine, published February 18, 2000, points out the adaptability and remarkable survival qualities of crocodiles. The article discusses a group of crocodiles that live in caves in the Sahara Desert and serve as tropical relics that have managed to survive for thousands of years in isolation from other crocodile populations.

> [Zoologist] Wolfgang Bohme of . . . Bonn, Germany, and his team found a population of Nile crocodiles during a reptile study of the western Sahara. Hearing of an enigmatic crocodile colony in southern Mauritania, they traveled to a large rocky plateau ruptured by crevices and cavities. There, some 5 meters down, they saw water and found an underground pond about 20m wide containing four adult crocodiles. The adults were about 2m long, compared to up to 6m for other Nile crocodiles.

keep moisture under and around them. While crocodiles estivate, other creatures such as frogs and crabs burrow down with them and are protected by their large bodies.

All of these unique characteristics have aided the crocodile's survival for eons. Its physiology, carnivorous diet, and habitat preferences saw it through several ice ages and the movement of continents, and the crocodiles alive today are excellent replicas of their ancient ancestors.

2

Crocodile Hunting

DURING THE MIDDLE part of the twentieth century, hunting severely reduced the world's crocodile population. Many species neared extinction after they were overexploited for their skins. Crocodiles' scaly skin is not like the skin of other reptiles. The animals do not molt like snakes; their skin grows as they grow. The only way to get a complete crocodile skin is to kill a crocodile. Although in smaller numbers, crocodiles are still killed today for their skins, for food and ritual, and also because many people simply do not like the animals.

Crocodiles as commerce

The crocodile-skin business has become an important part of international commerce. According to one conservation group, international trade in all crocodilian (including alligator and caiman) skins is worth $500 million annually.

Much of the development of this industry began in the early twentieth century, when tourism increased in remote areas of the world. Safaris had been popular adventure trips since the early 1800s, and as transportation became more sophisticated, more and more people began taking extended hunting trips into primitive areas. The killing of large crocodiles as trophies became a sport, and many adult animals were slaughtered for this purpose.

It quickly became evident to the people who lived in these safari regions that they could make money by displaying and selling crocodile heads, teeth, and bones. They also made items from the skins, including hat and wrist bands, key chains, and pouches. They began killing the crocodiles just to get body parts to make these novelties. For hunters from impoverished rural villages, selling these items provided welcome extra income.

Improvements in transportation during the 1800s made travel into remote areas of the world and hunting crocodile for sport popular.

The crocodile craze

The popularity of the exotic items led to larger displays and buyers coming from cities around the world to stock

their shops. Designers created expensive handbags and shoes, lamp shades, and other furnishings using the popular skins. Those industries produced a great amount of revenue. For example, a crocodile skin might be bought from a native hunter for $200, but a wallet made from a small part of that skin would sell in Paris for $150 ($100 more than the same design made out of cowhide). And one average-size crocodile skin could easily become six to ten wallets.

By the mid–twentieth century, then, world urban communities had developed a fondness for items fashioned from animal pelts. The skins of crocodiles and alligators were used to make everything from shoes to home furnishings. High-fashion marketplaces around the world developed extensive lines of handbags, shirts, belts, wallets, and more. Located primarily in France, Italy, the United States, and Hong Kong, these large-scale operations required tens of thousands of crocodilian skins each year from which to make their products. Thus, crocodile hunting became a specialized business.

Natives living in crocodile habitats quickly capitalized on the growing demand for crocodile skins.

Methods for hunting crocodiles

The methods hunters use to trap and kill crocodiles vary depending on location and the intended use of the animal. Professional skin hunters who want a whole crocodile hide to sell to tanneries most often bait traps with poisoned meat that will kill the crocodile without leaving any marks on the hide. This method also saves the hunter from having to get close to the live animal. Several traps can be set throughout the crocodile habitat, and the hunters check these traps on a regular basis. The dead animal will be skinned right there, and the hunter will take only the skin, head, and claws, the parts he can sell.

Another method is to stretch a strong net in the trees above a crocodile's path. When the animal comes into the area, it trips a wire and the net falls on top of it. The people who set the trap then kill the animal with blows to its head or with harpoons. This style of hunting is most often done when people are hunting crocodiles for their meat.

Shooting crocodiles with rifles is also effective. Many crocodiles are nocturnal, preferring to search for prey or be on land during the cooler night hours of their tropical habitats. Crocodiles' eyesight is quite good in the dark. Their eyes are immobile spheres with vertical pupils that dilate to improve vision. A layer of membranes, called tapetum, at the back of their eyes also increases night vision. But at night, the tapetum reflects light and makes crocodiles' eyes appear red. From a boat, it is very easy to shine a bright light along the swamps or riverbanks and then shoot the animals between their glowing red eyes. This is an easy, low-risk way to harvest a lot of crocodiles in a short amount of time. It is also a method employed to rid an area of crocodiles that are considered dangerous to humans.

Destruction of crocodile populations

It is difficult to determine the exact number of crocodiles that were killed for their skins because the statistics used to

Because they are nocturnal animals, crocodiles are easy to locate at night using bright lights.

show the decline of populations are about all crocodilians, not just crocodiles. According to a statement in *Oneworld* magazine, an ecologically oriented on-line website with information about conservation and world environment, in a fifty-year period (1930–1980) more than 20 million crocodilians were killed for their skins. But since crocodiles make up fourteen of the twenty-three crocodilian species, most researchers believe it is reasonable to assume that crocodile deaths accounted for more than half of the 20 million killed.

Because crocodiles were extensively killed to supply the leather market, crocodile species with valuable skins were more sought after than others. Crocodiles form bony consistencies in their scales, called osteoderms. This is what gives crocodiles the protective armor that covers them. Skins with a lot of osteoderms are tough and hard to tan into leather. Thus, hunters prefer crocodile species with few osteoderms because hides of these species are easier to process into leather.

An example of this is the estuarine crocodile, which is the world's largest species and is found throughout Asia, the Indo-Pacific, and the wetlands of Australia. Estuarines have few osteoderms, which makes them valuable for the leather trade. According to Adam Britton, a leading crocodilian researcher,

> Between 1945 and the late 1960s, salties [estuarine crocodiles] were hunted so intensively for their scaly coats that populations throughout northern Australia were pushed to dangerously low levels. . . . Fewer than 3,000 crocodiles were estimated to remain out of a former population of close to 100,000.[2]

The Nile crocodile, the world's second-largest crocodile species, is also valued for its skin, which has few osteoderms. The skin is highly durable and ranges in color from drab green or brown to a blackish tone on the back (the dorsal side) and is much lighter and softer on the belly (ventral) surface. The Nile crocodile is found throughout western and central Africa. In the Okavango region of Botswana, one of Africa's last great wildlife refuges, hunting between 1950 and 1975 reduced the area's Nile crocodile population by four-fifths.

Early conservation efforts

By the mid-1960s many people around the world became more interested in conservation and animal rights. Because of this, a major outcry against the use of animal skins in the fashion and home furnishing industries came

The estuarine crocodile is the world's largest crocodile species, and its skin is considered extremely valuable in the leather trade.

from residents of urban countries such as the United States and Australia and the nations of Europe. This spurred action and protest in these areas, and crocodile conservation began.

In the United States, crocodiles benefited quite early when protection was given to the American alligator. In Florida (the only state in which American crocodiles are found), alligators and crocodiles share the same habitats, and hunting alligators for their skins was an important part of commerce there. Crocodiles, though, were often killed by hunters who thought they were killing alligators. The alligator populations suffered so much from being hunted for their skins that laws were passed in 1954 outlawing the hunting of alligators. These restrictions also kept crocodiles from being killed.

Gary Zillfeisch and the Hartley's Creek Zoo

In Australia, the uncontrolled killing of two crocodile species, the estuarine crocodile and the freshwater crocodile, greatly concerned a private citizen named Gary Zillfeisch. Thus, Zillfeisch began special efforts to save the wild population of crocodiles. He owned a popular roadside attraction in Queensland called Hartley's Creek Zoo and began offering hunters twice as much for a live crocodile as they would get for the animal's skin. Zillfeisch kept the crocodiles he bought in enclosures at the zoo. His efforts attracted interest from around the world, and many documentaries about crocodiles were produced at his establishment. This international interest and education helped persuade the Queensland government to legislate all crocodiles as a protected species in 1972.

More support for conservation

Commercial hunters also became eager to support crocodile protection programs. These hunters realized that their bounty had been seriously reduced by overhunting. Because so many adult crocodiles had been killed for their skins, there were not enough of the animals left to replenish the dwindling populations. Crocodiles had to be protected or the hunters would soon lose their source of revenue.

The hunters' concerns were a major reason the British colony of Rhodesia (now the country of Zimbabwe) gave legal protection to crocodiles in the 1960s. Both the dwarf crocodile, which is hunted for its meat, and the Nile crocodile, which is greatly desired for its skin, live in this area, and local hunters relied on income made from killing these crocodiles. As far as the hunters in this and other regions were concerned, the need to have regulations was important so that the species and the commerce they produced would continue.

International protection

Finally, in 1971, the plight of crocodiles was highlighted worldwide. That year, the International Union for the Conservation of Nature (IUCN) listed all crocodilian species as endangered, threatened, or declining in numbers.

The IUCN had initiated its first list of endangered plants and animals eight years earlier. The species identified by this list had been reported by researchers as disappearing from their native habitat or becoming threatened by human development. Appendix I of the list became known as the Red List, for critically endangered species, and Appendix II is for those species that are vulnerable to becoming endangered. In 1971 all crocodiles were listed in those two appendixes.

The IUCN took the protection of crocodiles and other endangered species one step further when it established the Convention on International Trade in Endangered Species of Wild Fauna and Flora (CITES). With support from other international organizations and national governments, this special international treaty regulated the trade and commerce of all endangered species identified by Appendixes I and II and prohibited the international sale of skins from endangered or potentially endangered animals. CITES also required government permits for any trading of crocodile skins and proof that the skins were legal had to be written on special types of paper with official stamps to prevent forgery.

Every nation in the world was invited to participate in the CITES treaty, and by 1973 nearly one hundred countries, including most of the countries that housed the big leather industries that made items from crocodile skins, had signed the treaty. This effort greatly reduced the large-scale hunting of crocodiles.

Problems persist

Although the development of CITES greatly improved crocodile recovery, the killing did not stop entirely. One hundred fifty-two countries have signed the CITES treaty, but nine African countries, seven countries in the Americas, and twelve in Asia did not sign the CITES treaty until the 1990s. The two decades of continued crocodile killing in these places further reduced certain crocodile populations.

Updating the Red List Criteria

The International Union for the Conservation of Nature (IUCN), which in 1971 listed all crocodiles as endangered and threatened, is one of the world's oldest conservation organizations. Established in 1948 as the World Conservation Union, its goals, as stated on the IUCN website, are "to influence, encourage, and assist societies throughout the world to conserve the integrity and diversity of nature."

The IUCN developed a list of criteria regarding threatened crocodiles and other species in 1963. The criteria included definitions of the terms *extinction* and *endangerment.* In 1994 the IUCN updated these criteria to include a status of "extinct in the wild," to be assigned when a species is known to survive only in captivity or in naturalized populations well outside of their former habitat. The Siamese crocodile is one species that falls into this category.

At the same time, another criterion was defined: "data deficient," to be assigned when researchers are unable to determine the range of habitat and population of a species. Crocodiles such as Morelet's crocodile, the false gharial, and slender-snouted crocodile have this distinction.

The slender-snouted crocodile has been assigned the status of "data deficient" by the IUCN.

Because of this, the IUCN status of the American crocodile, for example, which can be found in the largest numbers along the Pacific and Atlantic coastlines of sixteen equatorial countries, was upgraded from threatened to critically endangered.

Furthermore, not all countries that are home to crocodiles participate in the CITES agreement. The crocodile skins that come from these non-CITES nations are often sold to small leather manufacturers that do not follow international trade rules. Other skins might be marketed in the country where the crocodiles were killed, where the leather merchants are not required to provide proof of where the leather came from. Together, these actions contribute to the world's ever-dwindling crocodile populations.

The U.S. Fish & Wildlife Service has seized many illegal crocodile skins at U.S. ports of entry. This display is part of a touring exhibit called "Confiscated" which presents a sampling of those skins.

Poaching

In the CITES countries, poaching of crocodiles is also a big problem. Poaching can include the illegal sale of live animals as well as the killing of animals for illegal skin

trade. In a few Asian and African countries, for instance, an illegal market exists to provide live juvenile crocodiles for private farms and parks. In the waterways near Myanmar, a Southeast Asian country that prohibits such trade, locals reported that buyers in fishing boats regularly purchased live juvenile and adult crocodiles.

Because crocodile habitats are often remote, it is difficult to stop the illegal killing and unauthorized trade of crocodile skins. To do so would require a great number of people to check documentation and monitor activity along rivers and lakes where crocodiles live. Many countries simply do not have enough money to do this and can hire only a few conservation officials. In these areas, problems abound. Forgery of CITES stamps and papers, for example, is not always detected.

Early in 1999 Andrew Eriksen, who owns a legally established crocodile ranch in South Africa, commented on an illegal crocodile skin trading network established on the island of Mauritius in the Indian Ocean:

> I recently traveled to Mauritius [which did not sign the CITES treaty until 1998] and found large quantities of crocodile skin products in the shops and market places there. All were Nile crocodile skins and most of the items made included the back skin. The processing was obviously not done in a tannery. I established from the La Vanille Crocodile farm on the Island, that these skins were arriving in Mauritius illegally from Madagascar [which outlawed crocodile hunting in 1975].[3]

Situations like this one are common. Often, the enforcement of CITES regulations takes place only at government borders and international ports of entry. However, there are many border crossings that are not monitored, particularly in certain mountainous regions, and it is quite easy for poachers to bypass controls and enter countries illegally in those spots.

Other reasons crocodiles are killed

Although it is probably the most well-known reason, the killing of crocodiles is not done just for their commercial value. They have, for example, long been hunted as a local food source. The animals provide meat rich in protein and have pockets of fat that are used in cooking, preserving meats, and lubricating ropes and leather. The shy dwarf crocodile is one species that has been extensively hunted for its meat in the Congo and Cameroon—two of the twenty East African countries where it is found. Scientists estimate that tens of thousands of dwarf crocodile are sold annually for consumption in these areas.

Not all crocodiles are hunted for commercial reasons. The dwarf crocodile is one species that has long been hunted for its meat rather than its skin.

Crocodiles are also killed for cultural purposes, mainly ceremonies that local human populations have participated in for centuries. Historically, animals would be killed for

inclusion in burial sites of kings or to make amulets for warding off evil. Today in some regions of the Americas, Africa, and Asia, certain crocodile body parts are considered to have medicinal value or magical qualities. Native people also use crocodile parts for decorations on ceremonial accessories and in sacrificial rites.

A dangerous species

Food and cultural uses for crocodile parts contribute to the animals' problematic situation. Such methodological practices almost guarantee that crocodiles in some parts of the world will be threatened. However, there is a less methodical, more random, contributor as well.

A great number of crocodiles are killed by people out of fear and loathing. James Perran Ross, coordinator of one crocodile conservation group, states, "Crocodiles pose some difficult problems for conservationists. The larger species in particular are usually regarded as dangerous and unattractive by people who have to live near them."[4]

Threats to farming and fishing

The animals threaten human livelihood in several ways. For instance, many people who reside in regions where crocodiles live depend on farming and fishing to feed their families. These people feel a real threat from the presence of an animal regarded by many as a fearsome predator. In Africa, one farmer reported an annual loss of 150 head of cattle to Nile crocodiles. People who have small ranches in the Indo-Pacific region have similar problems with estuarine crocodiles. Because these large crocodiles will attack domestic animals as prey, most people from the region feel justified in killing any crocodile on sight, even if it is not the species that has been depleting their stock and even if it is endangered or threatened.

For communities that rely on fishing, the threat from crocodiles is equally great. Crocodiles damage nets and fishing weirs, and they are a danger to the people who come to the water to fish. Furthermore, since the crocodiles' main diet is made up of fish, the animals are also

A Disliked Animal

Human attitudes and fears create serious problems for crocodile conservation. Many people who live near crocodile habitats do not like the animals. An article in the July–September 1999 on-line *Crocodile Specialist Group Newsletter*, entitled "Woman, 70, Killed by Crocodile in Jamaica," illustrates one reason for that dislike.

> Linda Atkinson, 70, the owner of a shop and bar in southwestern Jamaica, was swept into the Black River Wednesday by a crocodile witnesses described as about 10 feet (3 meters) long. Fishermen wrestled her away from the crocodile but she was pronounced dead at a hospital, police said.
>
> The incident angered residents in the area, who say crocodiles in the Black River are dangerous and should be killed.

Similar incidents occur in most regions where crocodiles live. As a result, the human attitude about crocodile conservation, especially among people living near crocodile habitats, is often very poor.

considered competition for the resources of the river or lake and are killed anytime they are found in good fishing areas. In a report from the Lake Stephanie area of Ethiopia, one official says, "[Nile] crocodiles are killed whenever they are sighted along this river which is quite shallow and wide. The locals do not tolerate the crocodiles and it seems their future is threatened along this river."[5]

Dangers to human life

Another reason people kill crocodiles has to do with the animals' continual threat to humans. Any carnivore is dangerous, but when one can outweigh a human by four times and also lurk silently in the mud and shadows, it is only natural for people to be defensive. Each year thousands of attacks and hundreds of deaths occur from estuarine crocodiles in Asia and the Indo-Pacific. American crocodiles cause deaths in Central America, and in Africa, Nile crocodile attacks are the second-biggest animal threat to people, after the hippopotamus.

Several human deaths resulting from crocodile attacks in Costa Rica has increased unauthorized crocodile killing by the local people. According to an article in the January–March 1999 *Crocodile Specialist Group Newsletter* entitled "Crocodile Situation Deteriorates in Tarcoles River" by Juan R. Bolanos, head of a Costa Rican crocodile protection agency,

> Just over this last Easter week, 5 adult crocodiles (average length 3.5 m) were killed, three decapitated and with the tail removed, one skinned and one killed in a fishing net at the river mouth, all in the Rio Tarcoles National Park. . . . Crocodiles are completely protected in Costa Rica but some recent human fatalities have aroused the population against them and appeals to the authorities to enforce the law have been ineffectual.[6]

Crocodiles sometimes do attack humans. For that reason, warning signs, such as these near the Adelaide River in Australia, have been posted in many places around the world.

Such a response is not uncommon. In Zambia, Africa, several hundred Nile crocodiles were targeted as vicious and undesirable. The threat to humans going to rivers to get water or wash clothes became so severe that the government authorized local hunters to get rid of the problem crocodiles, stating, "Human life is more important than that of any wild animal that threatens or kills human beings."[7]

Episodes like these only make the crocodiles' situation more precarious. Despite the fact that international laws have outlawed crocodile killing in most countries, poaching, hunting crocodiles where it is not banned by law, and the intentional, random killing of crocodiles continue anyway. And these circumstances further endanger several crocodile species.

3

Habitat Loss

ALTHOUGH THE COMMERCIAL hunting of crocodiles for their skins forced the animals close to extinction during the 1970s, today's major threat is the reduction of proper habitat. The habitats where crocodiles live are being altered and destroyed by commercial development, pollution, and natural disasters. As a result of this decline in tropical wetlands, crocodiles are being crammed into smaller areas. This severely threatens their population and is pushing some species toward extinction.

Threatened habitats

Crocodiles live in wetlands or swampy areas, along the earth's equator. Historically, these areas provided everything the animals needed to survive, but recently, these regions are changing at an alarming rate. According to one conservation organization, "Half of the world's wetlands have been drained, destroying habitat."[8] This means that crocodiles do not have as much living space as they once had.

It has been only recently that people have realized how important wetlands are to a region's ecosystem. According to Wetlands International, an international organization concerned with the conservation of wetlands and wetland species,

> Wetlands . . . help reduce the frequency, level and velocity of floods and riverbank erosion. They act as natural sponges that absorb floodwater, and help protect adjacent and downstream areas from flood damage. Many wetlands also help recharge

groundwater aquifers [the sand and stone underground that hold groundwater] by holding water and allowing it to infiltrate the ground slowly.[9]

Disappearing rain forests and coastal habitats

Rain forests, specifically, contain a great deal of wetlands. These areas are vital to the environment; they help protect the earth's atmosphere. But they are also quickly disappearing. Today rain forests cover only about 6 percent of the earth's land surface, less than half of what they covered in the late 1800s. Nearly 71 million acres of rain forest—an area about half the size of the state of Florida—are

With laws in place to help protect them from hunters, the biggest threat crocodiles face today is the destruction of their habitats by development, pollution, and natural disasters.

An Environmental Problem

The increase in pollution is a growing problem in all areas of the world, causing certain ecosystems to dwindle. This article, entitled "Brazil Oil Spill," from the January 22, 2000 issue of *USA Today,* is one example of how human activities are threatening the environment.

> A huge oil spill spreading across Guanabara Bay [Brazil] has reached ecologically vital mangrove swamps, threatening endangered animal species. Globo television [the region's leading television news source] said the 130,000 gallons of crude oil that gushed from a broken refinery pipeline has covered 16,000 square miles. Environmental officials said the leak was caused because state-owned oil company Petrobras' pipelines were old and poorly maintained.

destroyed each year. At this rate, researchers estimate that there will be no forests at all by the year 2035. According to the World Wildlife Fund, the most endangered rain forests are those in West Africa and in central and Southeast Asia. These are also the areas with the largest populations of crocodiles.

Coastal wetlands (mangrove swamps and salt marshes) are also rapidly diminishing. Since the 1920s, Myanmar (formerly Burma), for instance, one of Asia's largest countries, has drastically depleted its mangrove swamps. According to a report from one conservation group, "The [Myanmar] Forestry Department estimates that [the amount of] mangrove forest left in 1995 was 17% of 1925 levels and is highly degraded."[10]

Why habitats are disappearing

Reasons for those disappearing habitats are many. The most pressing, however, is an increasing world population that demands more land on which to grow crops and to build. Many of the wetlands inhabited by crocodiles were formerly thought of as wasteland or were too difficult to

Rain Forests

The trees of the rain forests play a vital role in producing the abundant rainfall these areas receive. In some places, the trees are so tall and the canopy of leaves so thick that rain barely reaches the ground as it falls. Instead, the water trickles down tree branches and stems and is eventually absorbed by the soil. A tree's roots then absorb most of this water and transport it more than two hundred feet up its trunk and back to its leaves. As the tree's leaves respire, or breathe, they release the moisture again as a gas that eventually evaporates and forms clouds.

It is estimated that these clouds contain more than 264 billion gallons of water. This water falls as rain, and the whole process begins again. Rain forests in New Zealand and New Guinea are considered some of the wettest places on the earth, with more than 250 inches of rain falling each year.

build on. But as the populations in these areas increase, people are finding new ways to change wetlands for human use. Rivers, for example, have been straightened and their marshy banks have been drained and lined with concrete, an act that decreases water flow and raises the water temperature.

Developers also often find that they use up or alter the makeup of much of the freshwater sources in these areas. In fact, in the tropical wetlands around the globe, a great deal of freshwater has been diverted for irrigation projects. One study conducted by the United Nations Development Programme has determined that humans now use more than half of the available freshwater in the world, with 70 percent of that going to agriculture.

Freshwater is also used to create electrical power. Hydroelectric plants have been built throughout the world and are particularly popular in developing nations where other fuels are scarce or too expensive. An example of this can be seen along the lower region of the Nile Valley of Egypt, where dams and dikes have been built since the late nineteenth century. These projects were an effort to prevent flooding and to provide irrigation and power to the large human population in and around Cairo.

Building hydroelectric plants has damaged these areas considerably and made them inhospitable to crocodiles and animals of all kinds. Pollutants resulting from increased industry after Egypt's Aswan High Dam was built in 1959, for example, nearly eradicated all wildlife from the area of the Nile below Cairo.

Pollution released into the Nile River after the construction of Egypt's Aswan High Dam in 1959 nearly wiped out all wildlife along the Nile near Cairo.

Slash and burn

Logging and clearing rain forests for development also destroy crocodile habitats. Using a technique called slash and burn, developers are cutting down the trees and creating,

out of the world's rain forests and wetlands, areas that can be put to use for humans. Eliminating the trees, though, opens the ground to sunlight and wind. Any moist soil and marshland quickly dries. Grass replaces the trees, and the open land can then be used as pastures for cattle to graze. Much of this land is near rivers or streams—areas that are also often crocodile habitats—so the cattle will have access to water.

The felled trees are then used as fuel for the local populations. Karen Free, an editor with *Habitat World,* writes,

> In developing countries, about 2 billion people rely solely on fuel wood as their energy source for heating and cooking. Traditional fuels, mostly firewood, supply about 52 percent of all energy required in sub-Sahara Africa. Forests are being cut down faster than they can grow, partly to make room for new farmland and partly to harvest trees as fuel.[11]

Rain forest trees that are not destroyed by slash-and-burn projects or cut for fuel usually become part of commercial logging operations. At least 11 million acres of wood are logged from rain forests each year. Teak, mahogany, and ebony are just a few of the valuable rain forest woods that are cut and sold in markets around the world. Many of the countries that supply the wood have few other economic resources, so they depend on logging to provide much-needed employment opportunities.

Problems for crocodiles

These human enterprises threaten and create problems for crocodile populations. As humans encroach on crocodile habitats, the animal's numbers decline. According to one conservation report, "Because [crocodiles] are quite large animals and because crocodiles increase through several orders of magnitude of size as they grow from hatchling to adult, they require areas of habitat that are both large and diverse."[12] Destruction of the tropical wetlands, however, means smaller habitats and nesting areas for crocodiles.

Crocodiles, though, are historically very adaptable. When their habitats shrink, they simply move. But today, many of the regions they move to already have crocodile

Clearing trees in rain forests to make way for construction destroys the crocodiles' habitats and endangers their future.

populations. This often leads to food shortages and even more space problems, leaving the crocodiles nowhere else to go. The mugger and estuarine crocodiles who live on the small Indo-Pacific island of Java face this problem. Dwindling habitat and food sources on the island are threatening their existence.

Likewise, crocodiles living in the Upper Nile wetlands, an area stretching from central Sudan south to the Uganda border, find themselves with less land to live on. Historically, the area has not been hospitable to human development, but in the twenty-first century the region saw an increase in the building of irrigation canals to support agricultural projects. The canals have drained many areas,

If Nile crocodiles such as this one do not get enough to eat, they will not grow as large or as quickly as they should.

including 11,580 square miles of swampland known as the Sudd, a crocodile habitat. As a result, the more than eighty thousand Nile crocodiles that live there face a drop in the number of waterways available for them to hunt in, a fact that, researchers contend, may lead to a dramatic drop in population. Nile crocodiles, like all other crocodile species, do not develop well if they don't get enough to eat. They don't grow as large as they need to or as quickly. Thus, because crocodile reproduction depends not only on the age but the size of the animal, many species simply cannot replenish their populations.

Irrigation and dams threaten young crocodiles

Besides threatening crocodile reproduction by keeping the animals from growing large enough to breed, the reduction of riverbank and marshlands has other effects. One is that the nesting of crocodiles, such as the New

Specialized Trees

On sheltered seashores along the equator, many of the muddy marshlands are called mangrove swamps. The swamps get their name from the mangrove trees that grow there. These trees are evergreens that have adapted to the swamps' salty conditions. More than sixty species of mangrove trees have evolved to survive in the different types of brackish (salty) waters around the world. The eastern mangrove forests, for instance, extend from Asia to East Africa, and the western mangrove forests are found along the coasts of the Americas and West Africa. The quick-growing trees are also beneficial in that they help prevent coastal erosion, and their hard wood is useful for construction and fuel.

The unique roots of the mangrove form slender outgrowths from the main trunk, known as prop roots, which develop their own root systems and support the tree in the soft mud. Another type of root allows the trees to breathe. Called pneumatophores, these roots poke up out of the mud and allow oxygen to reach the tree. The mangrove roots also collect mud that gradually builds up as banks, which ultimately dry out and create new ground. The country of Bangladesh, for example, has evolved primarily from the mangrove trees' ecosystem and contains the largest mangrove swamp in the world.

These mangrove trees are located in Key West, Florida.

Guinea crocodile, which lives in New Guinea, and the Siamese crocodile, found in Thailand and other Southeast Asian countries, is often disrupted as water is used for irrigation and as the level and flow of rivers changes due to the opening and closing of dams. When the river waters are raised, for instance, a nest originally built on a muddy shore can become completely submerged, drowning the crocodile embryos.

In India, changes in water level also threaten mugger crocodile hatchlings. Although the adults of this species have adapted well to reservoirs, irrigation canals, and man-made ponds, the tremendous changes in water levels make it difficult for the females to stay near their nests and protect their eggs from predators like jackals, boars, hyenas, and monitor lizards. Furthermore, large sections of the banks are often covered with concrete, and the hatchlings that do survive are too small to negotiate the steep artificial banks to reach the vegetation above. Thus, a large majority of the baby mugger crocodiles die in their first few weeks.

Young Nile crocodiles in Natal, South Africa, are also suffering as a result of irrigation projects. The water from Lake Saint Lucia is being piped upstream to irrigate large fields of maize. As the water level has decreased, the lake has become increasingly salty. Adult crocodiles have special glands in their mouths that collect salt from brackish waters; they then expel the salt when on land and it does not get into their system. But it takes several years for these glands to develop enough to perform efficiently, and young crocodiles must live in freshwater until then. Thus, the decrease of freshwater in Lake Saint Lucia and the rise of salt in the habitat increases the already-high mortality of infant crocodiles.

Pollution

An increase in the salt levels of those rivers is a form of pollution. Since the 1950s, development has polluted crocodile habitats in other ways as well, namely with natural and industrial waste. In highly populated areas such as

Southeast Asia, sewage is dumped into major rivers and streams, creating waste pollution. In countries that have many large livestock farms, such as South Africa and Mexico, the runoff from the animal pens also pollutes the water with waste. Introducing these types of waste causes bacteria growth, which spreads over green plants and uses up the oxygen in the water. This suffocates aquatic animals and destroys the water system's native plants. Further, industrial runoff, such as oils and metallic toxins like mercury—from factories, for example—also pollutes the water and kills aquatic life.

Agricultural pollutants

Agricultural pollutants, too, are destructive to crocodile habitats. When pesticides to kill insects and herbicides to reduce weeds are spread over crops, the chemicals settle into the soil and eventually leach into the nearby water systems. The pollution changes the temperature of the water and can reduce the fish population.

Pesticides used in crop dusting contribute to the pollutants contaminating crocodile habitats.

In some parts of the world, the pesticide DDT is used, primarily to reduce the threat of malaria by killing mosquitoes in swampy areas. DDT does not dilute in water, and it is known to be poisonous to the reproductive system of many vertebrates, particularly egg-laying animals like crocodiles. In South Africa, researchers are studying the effect this pesticide has on the wetlands of the Sibabya Lake area where Nile crocodiles live. The scientists suspect that DDT and other pesticides reduce the crocodiles' reproduction rates because the poisons effect the thickness of their egg shells and the proper development of the crocodile embryos.

Agricultural chemicals present problems other than water damage as well. When crocodiles eat contaminated fish or other prey, for instance, the toxins from those animals enter the crocodiles' bodies, often poisoning them or making them vulnerable to disease. The American crocodile in

Polluted water is particularly hazardous to crocodiles because they both live in the contaminated water and feed on animals that live there.

Florida is one species that is threatened by such contamination. Mercury runoff from agricultural plants has greatly reduced the fish populations in this habitat.

Waste from mining operations in the rain forests of Africa and South America has damaged crocodile habitats there. The sulfur dioxide, arsenic, and other toxins used in the mining process pollute the soil and water, and often the minerals being mined, such as uranium or copper, are toxic themselves; releasing these substances from the rocks in which they are imbedded pollutes the area. Smokestacks associated with smelters and the disposal of water used in the mining process also harm the environment when the acids and other toxins are released into the air and then leach into the soil. Eventually these pollutants reach larger streams and rivers, killing fish and destroying vegetation. As a result, the crocodiles that live along these water sources often die of starvation or mineral poisoning.

Commercial fishing

Pollutants such as these pose a considerable threat to the world's crocodile populations. However, another problem, commercial fishing, also puts crocodiles at risk. Commercial fishing harms crocodiles because it alters their habitats in several ways. One way is by damming or netting off water sources in an effort to keep fish contained and to prevent large animals, such as crocodiles, from threatening the fish. Another way is by depleting an area of its fish supply, thereby causing the crocodiles that live there to starve. By far, though, the predominant way commercial fishing threatens the world's crocodile populations is through the use of fishing nets. These nets are stretched across rivers or lakes in an attempt to capture large numbers of fish. The nets are generally made of extremely strong finely spun metal or monofilaments (synthetic threads). And when the nets become damaged or are no longer in use, they are usually abandoned in the waterway, creating hazards for crocodiles.

Crocodiles then become entangled in those nets, whether discarded or in use. The mesh is too small for a

Accidental Killings

Crocodiles often fall victim to human enterprises that are intended for other uses. One example of this is a fishing technique used in marshy areas of Africa and Asia. There, local fishermen make concoctions of narcotic herbs and pour the substance into a slow moving waterway. The herbs cause all aquatic life in the vicinity to become numb and unconscious, and the fishermen then can easily harvest the water's fish, shrimp, crab, and other marine life to be eaten or sold for profit. These small animals, however, often live in brackish waters and freshwater inlets of the world's equatorial areas, which are crocodile habitats.

The use of such fishing techniques causes much trouble for the crocodiles. Before the poison gets diluted in bigger waterways, many young crocodiles are rendered unconscious by the fishermen's drug. Sometimes the animals are swept away with the current. Others drown when they are trapped by debris at the water's edge. And still others get caught in the fishermen's nets and are usually killed. Furthermore, the shrimp and crabs taken from these waters serve as a crocodile food source. Without them, many crocodiles starve.

crocodile to push its snout through, and its thrashing is unable to rip the tough fiber. Often a crocodile will be trapped underwater by the net.

Being underwater is not usually a problem for crocodiles. They have the ability to stay submerged for twenty minutes or more while they search out food. Crocodiles can stay underwater this long because their heart is extremely efficient. The valves of the heart can redirect blood to essential body areas, which is an advantage when a crocodile is in a prolonged dive. The heart supplies oxygen only to the tissues that need oxygen for the dive, and a crocodile's heart rate can actually drop down to two or three beats per minute to help reduce oxygen consumption.

But when crocodiles become caught in fishing nets, sometimes half a day will pass before the nets are retrieved by fishermen, and the crocodiles drown. Even if some crocodiles manage to survive, they are usually in a state of shock and fishermen easily kill them.

Nile crocodiles in Kenya's Lake Turkana continually face this problem. The world's greatest concentration of wild crocodiles (more than eleven thousand) live along the northeastern shore of the lake. This lake is the largest alkaline lake in the world, measuring 165 miles long and an average of eighteen miles across, and it teems with fish. Palms, shrubs, and marsh plants grow along the lake's shore and make good places for crocodiles to nest. Nile crocodiles here have not been hunted much because the soapy-feeling waters of the lake ruin the crocodiles' skin for the leather market. But the lake is in a desert portion of Africa's Rift Valley and contains an abundant supply of

Many crocodiles, like this one in Lake Turkana, Kenya, are accidentally killed when they are caught in fishermen's nets and drown.

Nile perch and tilapias (a type of fish). These fish are of great value to the humans who live in the area, so daily, fishermen descend upon the lake and cast their nets into the water. Hundreds of crocodiles die each year when they become entangled in these fishing nets.

Flooding

Sometimes the results of these human-caused habitat problems (logging, pollution, lack of freshwater, commercial fishing) are made worse by natural threats, predominantly natural disasters. In the Indo-Pacific, for example, the months of July and August usually bring heavy rains and flooding to the lowlands of every country in the region. Because logging and development have destroyed many of the trees in the area, the flooding associated with this time period has increased in severity. According to one investigation, "With the clearing and levelling of coastal areas, such as those of Bangladesh, ecosystems and populations are becoming more vulnerable to flooding and tropical storms."[13] This directly affects crocodiles because crocodile nests are often totally submerged or destroyed by the force of the flood.

Natural disasters like Hurricane Mitch, which flooded this Central American settlement in 1998, are a threat to crocodiles because they also destroy crocodile habitats.

Crocodiles in Central and South America face a similar threat. Alteration of the rain forests there have greatly changed the flow of water and the ability of rivers to absorb great amounts of rainfall. Thus, flooding occurs more frequently. During periods of extreme floods, Orinoco crocodiles have traditionally left their homes along Venezuela's Orinoco River and traveled overland to nearby lakes and ponds, returning to the river when the rainy season ends. Recently, though, many have returned before the floodwaters recede, and the animals are swept to sea far away from their natural habitat.

Although natural disasters play only a secondary role, they do cause problems for crocodiles. These events, coupled with the continuing need of humans to use and alter the ecosystems crocodiles rely on to survive, have become the most severe threats to the continuation of all the crocodile species.

4

Crocodile Recovery

DURING THE 1970s, so many crocodile species were endangered or near the brink of extinction that special efforts had to be employed to save them. Motives for saving crocodiles varied, but the majority of efforts were geared, initially, toward providing skins for commercial profit.

Conservationists quickly realized, however, that wild crocodile populations were also in desperate need of new members. In parts of Africa, for instance, the Nile crocodile had been so depleted that a species of catfish called clarias was taking over the rivers and killing the perch and tilapias. Clarias were hunted only by the region's wild crocodiles. Thus, repopulating the crocodiles in those rivers was seen as an important conservation move. As a result, conservationists devised two related programs in an effort to combat the problems: catch-and-release programs and crocodile farms and ranches.

Catch and release

Catch and release is a program practiced worldwide and designed to breed threatened animals in captivity with the hopes of ultimately returning them to their wild habitat. Catch and release came about because, by 1973, the remaining number of breeding adult crocodiles in the wild was not enough to repopulate many areas naturally. Providing protected captive areas in which crocodiles could nest and hatchlings could grow would, conservationists hoped, help the animals recover.

The logistics of the program are fairly simple. Workers, primarily from national zoos or other private organizations, set up special crocodile confinements that simulate the animals' natural habitat. Within these confinements adult crocodiles are encouraged to nest and juvenile crocodiles can grow up safely. Ponds and pens are also constructed so the animals can swim and submerge; areas for basking and underbrush or shelters so the crocodiles can regulate their body temperature are provided as well. The animals are fed (usually chickens) by the facility workers and are frequently examined for signs of disease and illness. As the young crocodiles grow, they are placed in larger pens and ponds to accommodate their needs. After they have reached a healthy size and sufficient age, the young animals are released into natural habitats that can support them.

Saving endangered species

Many captive-breeding programs have been very successful. In the Philippines, for example, a program at the Crocodile Farming Institute, operated by the Philippine

Captive breeding is just one program used by zoos and private organizations to help preserve and protect crocodiles.

Chai Yai, listed in the Guinness Book of World Records *as the largest crocodile in captivity, lives on the Sumatprakarn Crocodile Farm in Thailand.*

government, is one of the last remaining hopes for the Philippine crocodile. The program began in 1989 with 204 animals that the staff acquired both from the wild and from private sources. According to an official survey released by one conservation group, "The captive stock has steadily increased from 265 (in 1992) . . . [to] 500 (in 1994) of which 33 were adult females producing eggs."[14]

In India, the catch-and-release plan has been even more successful. Populations of the area's mugger crocodile had been steadily declining. In 1975, though, the Indian government began a captive-breeding program. Initially, the project was embraced by the Indian people, many of whom consider crocodiles sacred. Since then, the juveniles raised in these facilities have been used to restock natural populations in twenty-eight national parks, wildlife reserves, and crocodile sanctuaries throughout the country. Adult crocodiles from India have also been supplied to breeding facilities in Pakistan, and since the 1990s nearly one thousand mugger crocodiles have been released from captive-breeding facilities into the protected reservoirs of India's Gir Forest.

Catch-and-release problems

This is not to say the programs are without problems. One enormous concern is where to release the young crocodiles. Many countries are running out of appropriate habitats that do not interfere with human needs. In India, for example, where captive breeding helped repopulate the wild mugger crocodile, people who live in the regions that are close to the crocodiles' habitats are becoming increasingly reluctant to

One of the problems with catch-and-release programs is that there are limited areas in which to release young crocodiles.

share space with the animals. Thus, in 1994 the Indian government had to instruct captive-breeding facilities not to produce any new offspring, and currently the captive-breeding program there is at a standstill.

This situation has particularly hurt Romulus Whitaker, an American who founded the Madras Crocodile Bank in India in 1975. This facility bred endangered crocodilians, primarily mugger crocodiles. For nearly twenty years, the Indian government bought young crocodiles from Whitaker to restock the crocodile population in the lakes and swamps of the Ganges Delta. However, the wild crocodile populations quickly increased, reducing the demand for animals raised in captivity, and in 1997 the government stopped buying Whitaker's crocodiles altogether. Due to national and international laws, though, the Indian government also would not let Whitaker sell the animals for their skins because crocodiles are listed as an endangered species in India. According to an article in the magazine *Times South Pacific,* "If Whitaker were to skin one of his own crocodiles, he would face three years in jail and a $650.00 fine."[15] Therefore, Whitaker owns more than three thousand crocodiles and has no market for them.

Farms and ranches

In addition to catch-and-release programs that focus mainly on restocking wild populations, conservationists have devised a way to meet the demands of a market that relies on crocodile parts, although their efforts also protect wild populations. Because commercial leather industries depend on crocodile skins and many other markets sell the animals' meat, farms and ranches have sprung up to produce crocodiles specifically for international trade. Farms and ranches are not only aids to commerce, but they also are, according to some modern environmentalists, valid conservation tools. Although farms and ranches can often be found operating within the same facility, they differ slightly in their approach.

Crocodile ranching is the raising in a controlled environment of eggs or hatchling crocodiles taken from the wild

A crocodile rests at a South African crocodile farm. Farms like this one help balance animal preservation with commercial needs.

for the purpose of commercial use. After several years the crocodiles are killed, and their meat and skins are sold to appropriate markets.

Farming, on the other hand, is the controlled breeding of crocodiles; eggs and young are raised at the facility. Adults of breeding age (seven to ten years and older), most often from crocodile ranches, breed and the females lay their eggs at the facility. Once the eggs have hatched and the youngsters reach the age when most researchers believe they can manage on their own (approximately six to nine months), the small creatures serve one of two purposes. They are either raised to adulthood at the farm for their skins and meat or they are sold to crocodile ranches for breeding purposes.

Early farming

Commercial farming and ranching of crocodilians started in the United States after the hunting of alligators—crocodiles' close cousins—was declared illegal in 1954. As a way to protect the successful businesses that had developed

Warmth Is Important for Egg Development

Farms and ranches often want different sexes of crocodiles. Male crocodiles are desirable because they become large and grow quickly. For commercial use, having male crocodiles means producing larger skins. Female crocodiles, on the other hand, are important to keep the breeding stock at quality numbers and guarantee new crops of eggs.

Fortunately, officials at farms and ranches have realized that the temperature at which a crocodile egg is incubated will determine the animal's sex. Crocodile eggs must be kept at temperatures between eighty-two and ninety-five degrees Fahrenheit. The higher the temperature, and especially if it is higher than eighty-seven degrees, the greater the chance the embryo will develop into a male. In this way, farms and ranches can breed the animals they need, thereby maintaining their populations.

around the harvest of alligator skins, alligator farms were established. At these farms, eggs taken from nests in the wild were kept in incubators until they hatched; the little alligators were then raised in captivity for use in the skin market. As a result, businesses still had alligator skins for commercial use—even though the laws made it illegal to kill wild alligators—and the wild population recovered.

A few years later, in 1961, crocodiles in Zimbabwe received similar legal protection. Consequently, many local hunters lost money, and the nation's overall trade income declined. To fix the problem, the government quickly began developing farms and ranches in an effort to restock wild populations, provide the market with skins, and protect its economy.

The idea becomes popular

The practice of farming and ranching crocodiles did not become popular worldwide until the 1970s, however. Up until that time, the killing of wild crocodiles was commonplace. Businesses got all of the skins they needed from wild populations.

But as environmentalists protested the dwindling numbers of wild crocodiles and countries made it illegal to kill them, more farms and ranches were developed to meet the commercial demand for crocodile skins. Today crocodile ranches and farms can be found in most countries that have crocodile habitats.

Farms aid recovery

For the most part, the efforts have been successful. In Australia, for example, commercial farming and ranching, combined with legal protection, has been so successful that

An employee works in the incubator room of the Baobab Crocodile Farm in Kenya. Facilities like this help maintain the crocodile population in the wild.

the wild crocodile population is maintaining an annual 6 to 8 percent increase even with the harvesting of more than ten thousand eggs per year. Estuarine crocodiles (or salties), for one, have made a notable recovery.

Salties are the largest crocodiles in the world. With a length of up to twenty-three feet and a durable, attractively patterned skin, they also have some of the most commercially valuable hides of any crocodilian. Because their re-

John F. Kennedy International Airport officials in New York display confiscated crocodile products. Because of legalized ranching and farming, scenes like this have become rare.

covery has been so complete, annual wild crocodile hunts are held in Australia, primarily on private lands. The hunts are closely regulated, though. All participants must have a special permit and each hunter is assigned a quota (the number allowed to be killed each year) to maintain a sufficient number of wild crocodiles.

In Australia and several other countries that have legalized crocodile ranching and farming, the illegal trading and poaching of crocodile skins has sharply declined. Tanzania officials, for instance, believe that by using skins from farms and ranches, the killing of wild Nile crocodiles for their skins will soon be stopped entirely.

Wild egg harvests

To maintain the successes of these programs (both ranching and captive breeding), the proper harvesting of eggs is critical. Egg harvests take place during the first month of the nesting season, which varies in different parts of the world and depends on climate and rainfall. In most subtropical regions, such as Africa and Australia, the nesting season is in October.

Crocodile Furnishings

The legal hunting of wild crocodiles in Australia has opened up a whole new commercial market for the use of crocodile skins. "Crocodile Chairs," an article in the *Crocodile Specialist Group Newsletter*, describes one way these skins are used: as a covering for chairs.

> An unusual offering of crocodile leather for furnishings was recently displayed in the USA . . . Louis Shanks Furniture in Austin, Texas . . . is stocking a new feature line of full size wing back chairs covered in crocodile skin. The chairs, constructed and finished by furniture manufacturer William Alan Ltd. of [South Carolina], are covered with single skins of "monster crocs" legally harvested from the wild in Australia.

Finding the nests can be difficult, especially along lakes and riverbanks that have a lot of soft soil or sand. For this reason, egg collectors must be aware of how the crocodiles like to build their nests. The collectors most often look for crocodile footprints or waste since many females of the larger species (the ones that are particularly desired for farms and ranches) stay near their nests throughout the incubation period. These signs show an area the animal has frequently visited, one that often conceals a nest.

Once they locate a spot that may be a nest, the egg collectors poke a long metal rod into the ground. They will know if the area hides a nest when they pull the rod out and it has remnants of eggshell and yoke on it. They then dig down to uncover the nest, take out a number of eggs, and carefully re-cover the remaining eggs.

As a protection to wild populations, more than 70 percent of the eggs are left in the nest to mature naturally. In the early days of farms and ranches, this was not always the case. Often nearly 80 percent of the eggs from one nest would be taken, and the eggs that remained would be eliminated by natural mortality, which includes birds and animals robbing the nest.

For the eggs they do take, collectors must pay special attention to the position of the egg. They have to lift the eggs carefully from the nest and mark an *X* on the top so that side of the egg will always be up; this is the part of the egg where the crocodile embryo is attached to the inside of the egg. If the egg is turned over, all of the fluids from the egg would flood that area and the embryo would never develop or hatch.

Reproduction concerns

Although there have been successes in the farming and ranching of crocodiles, problems do exist. One concern is the possibility of hybridization, which results from mating crocodiles from two different species. In these cases, the hatchlings are neither one species nor another but rather a blend.

Hybridization poses a considerable threat in Southeast Asia, where so few wild populations of the Siamese crocodile remain that the species is considered extinct. The populations of Siamese crocodiles that do exist live predominantly in captive-breeding facilities and crocodile farms. These facilities, though, have been mating the Siamese crocodile with the larger estuarine crocodile to produce an animal that is larger (pure Siamese crocodiles average only seven to nine feet) and has skin that results in higher commercial value. Although this crossbreeding has little effect on the estuarine crocodile, whose worldwide population is abundant, for the Siamese crocodile, whose population is small, hybridization just further reduces the number of this species.

Economic considerations

Another significant problem is the international economy. Commercial crocodile farms and ranches depend on the international market—the desire—for crocodile skins. In the mid-1990s the market slowed down—that is, the

Siamese crocodiles, like this one in the Miami Metro Zoo, are considered extinct because so few exist in the wild.

demand for crocodile skins decreased, and international manufacturers of purses, belts, and shoes experienced a decline in sales. Many farms, however, continued to produce young crocodiles at a steady rate, even though they had nowhere to sell them.

By 1995 the captive crocodile population at one Ethiopian farm had increased beyond the facility's capacity. Disease broke out among the animals, and the Crocodile Specialist Group, a crocodile conservation organization, was called on to help slaughter and market two thousand of the oldest animals and to propose a solution to crocodile health problems. According to J. Hutton of the Africa Resources Trust, a conservation organization, "The slaughtered animals realized a net profit of around $90,000, which, while only a third of their potential value, was a good return considering the extent of disease and injuries."[16]

A controversial solution

Problems such as hybridization, overcrowding, and threats of disease at some commercial farms and ranches have caused heated debate among conservationists. Some believe farms and ranches are necessary to preserve the species. Others contend that such facilities only promote behavior and an international market that will lead to endangerment. Adam Britton, a leading crocodilian scientist, is one researcher who advocates crocodile farms and ranches. He does not feel there would be support for crocodile conservation without them. Britton says,

> Even the very word "crocodile" carries enough emotional baggage to instill irrational fear and loathing into many. It is little surprise that cries of "save the crocodile!" usually go unheeded unless radical approaches [namely farms and ranches] are used.[17]

On the other hand, critics of these programs believe that perpetuating the commercial demand for skins is not an effective solution. In fact, activists like Australia's Steve Irwin, better known as "the Crocodile Hunter," believe farms only make things worse. According to Irwin,

> The TRUTH, the plain and simple truth is the fact that while these . . . farms continue to supply native wildlife products

Some conservationists feel that commercial farms and ranches are crucial to the preservation of crocodiles, but others believe they only perpetuate the demand for crocodile products.

> [skins to use for belts, shoes, etc.] then the demand will never cease. These farms are fuelling the market.[18]

Some researchers, though, believe that saving wild crocodile populations is all a matter of balance. One of Brazil's leading conservationists, William E. Magnusson, for instance, contends that the farms and ranches are beneficial only when they fit into an overall conservation plan that includes habitat protection and returning animals to the wild:

> [A farm or ranch] is only valuable if it fits into an integrated plan. The idea that making a few people economically dependent on crocodilians will ensure the crocodiles survival is ludicrous. . . . Conservationists do use, and very much appreciate the support of farmers, ranchers, hunters and tanners. However the idea that we can then sit back and leave it up to those overworked businessmen to save [crocodile populations and] habitats for us is a sad dream.[19]

Many people share Magnusson's view, and those of Irwin and Britton. Thus, the debate over farms and ranches continues. In the meantime, the number of farms and ranches grows steadily, and today nearly two hundred facilities exist worldwide.

Crocodiles and tourism

In an effort to answer these critics and to increase income to local areas (both residents and corporations), many catch-and-release facilities, and crocodile farms and ranches have added a new feature to their establishments: tourism. By turning their facilities into private zoos or reptile parks, they have created more economic opportunities for the local people of their region, thereby boosting public support for crocodile conservation.

The farms offer various holding ponds and pens up for public viewing, and because the animals are always on display, the facilities are kept in excellent condition, which makes for healthy crocodiles. Many farms also have restaurants that serve crocodile meat, and those facilities that are connected with tanneries have gift shops where crocodile products can be purchased. Such tourist spots can be found in China, Thailand, Germany, Madagascar, Australia, and many other countries around the world.

The Crocodile Farm at Pierrelatte, France, is an example of such a place. The Crocodile Farm houses more than 350 crocodiles under a specially designed greenhouse. The facility is open daily throughout the year to visitors, and it has a sheltered picnic area, a bar, and a gift shop. The farm was originally developed as a catch-and-release facility whose purpose was to provide young Nile crocodiles for African countries wishing to reintroduce these animals

Steve and Terri Irwin

The famous pair of Steve and Terri Irwin were both born into families that encouraged conservation. An Australian native, Steve Irwin is best known for his lively television program, "The Crocodile Hunter," about animals and conservation. He has been involved in conservation all of his life. His parents are both respected naturalists in Australia, and at a young age Steve helped to feed and care for the animals at the family's Queensland Reptile and Fauna Park. Today he is the director of the Australia Zoo in Queensland, Australia, and he volunteers his services to the Queensland government's crocodile relocation program, where he catches troublesome crocodiles and moves them away from populated areas. Also called, "the Crocodile Hunter," Irwin has been the subject of several documentaries, the first of which was produced in 1992.

Terri Irwin (nee Raines) was born in Eugene, Oregon. Her father ran a successful construction business and was constantly bringing home injured creatures from the highways. Terri developed an ongoing commitment to save and rehabilitate wild animals, and in 1986 she started a facility called Cougar Country near her hometown to release animals such as foxes, raccoons, bears, bobcats, and cougars back into the wild. Soon she was handling three hundred animals a year.

During a 1991 trip to Australia to study the rehabilitation methods used in Australian wildlife parks, she met Steve Irwin. The couple married in June 1992. They have a daughter, Bindi Sue Irwin, born on July 24, 1998.

Terri and Steve Irwin pose with a nine-foot female alligator at the Australia Zoo in Queensland, Australia.

One of the most unique attractions in Europe, the Crocodile Farm in Pierrelatte, France, houses more than 350 crocodiles.

into their national parks and reserves. Today it is one of the most unique attractions in Europe.

Tourist spots like this are becoming popular worldwide as farms, ranches, and catch-and-release programs gain public attention. Despite the critics and the problems, such facilities are widely successful, and as a result, most crocodile species are enjoying population increases.

5

Protecting Wild Populations and Habitats

CROCODILES ENDURED GEOLOGICAL and environmental changes and continued much the same for 200 million years. But the twentieth century presented problems that surpassed all others: existing with modern man.

This is, in fact, a problem that affects all of the earth's plants and animals. Two time Pulitzer Prize–winner and leading Harvard researcher Edward O. Wilson states, "Biologists who explore biodiversity see it vanishing before their eyes . . . and generally agree that the rate of species extinction is now 100 to 1,000 times as great as it was before the coming of humanity."[20]

Yet humanity will also be what saves the vanishing species. Although most crocodile populations are no longer at the high risk they were in the early 1970s, a great amount of work for their continued survival will come from human efforts and programs.

The establishment of parks and reserves

One of the principal ways to aid crocodiles and all endangered species has been the establishment of protected areas, primarily national parks and reserves. National parks are large areas of land where human exploitation has not changed the landscape and flora and fauna indigenous to the area thrive and are cultivated. Reserves are smaller

At the Okavango Wildlife Reserve in northern Botswana, Africa, crocodiles can bask in the sun undisturbed by predators and humans.

areas set aside to protect certain species or habitats. Parks and reserves are normally open to the public and contain trails and areas for people to hike, camp, and observe wildlife. However, both parks and reserves also often have portions that are considered wildlife sanctuaries, places where human trespass is not allowed.

National parks and reserves are some of the best-protected areas for crocodiles. In these areas, the animals cannot be hunted, and the habitat is controlled or monitored. For crocodiles, this means they have large areas of wetlands where they can grow undisturbed. An example is the Okavango, a large wildlife reserve (four thousand square miles) in northern Botswana, Africa. This park provides protection for Nile crocodiles. Hundreds of miles of the eastern edge of Okavango are fenced to keep predators, including humans, out of the region.

Parks come in all sizes

The national parks and reserves where crocodiles live vary in size and location. The Serengeti National Park in Tanzania is one of the largest, covering fifty-seven hundred square miles. There, the Nile crocodile inhabits the marshes along the Mara River. The Serengeti also borders the thirty-two-hundred-square-mile Ngorongoro Conservation Area, which extends over part of East Africa's Rift Valley. Although grasslands abound here, this protected area also contains forests with ponds and lakes that are favored by the slender-snouted crocodile.

Other parks are quite small, such as the Royal Chitwan National Park in Nepal. At only 370 square miles, Royal Chitwan was the country's first national park, established in 1973. The mugger crocodile thrives in the flood plains of the three rivers that flow through the park. The swamps, marshes, and small lakes (called *tals*) of the flood plains are good breeding areas for the mugger, the only crocodile that lives in Nepal.

Problems in the park systems

In the parks' tropical sheltered areas, crocodiles live in an appropriate habitat and hunt and reproduce without harmful interference from humans. Not all restricted areas provide such protection, however. An example is in the country of Myanmar, where the Meinmahla Kyun Wildlife Sanctuary

This Nile crocodile rests safely on the shores on the Mara River in the Masai Mara Game Reserve in Kenya, Africa.

Charlie's Place

In 1934 a young crocodile was purchased for six dollars to star in an attraction called "the Best Crocodile Show in Australia." Pop Evans, who bought the animal and set up the show at his facility (which became Hartley's Creek Zoo), named the crocodile Charlie. Throughout Australia, Charlie's show was famous. In fact, Hartley's Creek Zoo was the first (and for many years the only) place in Australia where crocodiles performed for the public and were hand-fed.

In 1986 the Freeman family bought the zoo and made extensive renovations. They expanded the crocodile breeding program (begun in 1961) and reopened the zoo as the Hartley's Creek Crocodile Farm. Registered with CITES, the farm raises crocodiles for commercial use, is open to the public, and offers educational programs. Charlie, the crocodile bought in 1934 by the original owner, remained there through all of the changes and holds the record for being the crocodile held longest in captivity. Charlie died on September 17, 2000. He was estimated to be between seventy and eighty years old.

takes up most of Meinmahla Kyun Island in the lower Bogale River. The mangrove swamps and forests around the perimeter of the island are good habitats for crocodiles, and water access to the sanctuary is patrolled by the military. But there is also a human population that lives near the center of the island. Their land borders the sanctuary. The people on Meinmahla Kyun do not like the crocodiles. They are quick to destroy crocodile nests they find in the marshy areas where they grow rice, and they kill young crocodiles in the streams where they fish. This has affected the crocodile population in the sanctuary. A 1999 survey by the international Wildlife Conservation Society estimated "the number of adult crocodiles in the [Meinmahla Kyun Wildlife Sanctuary] at no more than 10 individuals and the total non-hatchling population [eggs] at no more than 100."[21]

Even with armed guards, the perimeters of Meinmahla Kyun, like those of most parks, are usually so extensive that it is difficult to keep people out. Poachers can easily gain access to these areas and kill crocodiles for food or body parts.

A need for more officials

Security concerns like this have prompted many countries to hire armed guards to patrol the grounds. In many places, though, it is extremely difficult for officials to cover all areas of the park. The security patrols are often short staffed, meaning the parks do not have enough guards and the laws designed to protect the areas cannot be enforced. According to one conservationist, "There are many countries that have good legislation, but lack the capacity to enforce it."[22]

Understaffed patrols have become a problem at parks in Central America. These parks, which total more than two hundred thousand square miles, have fewer than three

This park ranger keeps an eye on the land and animals at the Uluru National Park in Australia.

hundred officials to stop the illegal harvest of wild eggs, the poaching of adult American crocodiles for their skins, and the destruction of crocodile habitats.

Knowing no limits

The crocodiles themselves sometimes also make their situation worse. These animals do not know boundaries. They will often travel along a river to areas outside the reserve. Other times, they will walk into farming areas looking for food or better nesting places. When they do, they run the risk of being killed by humans who feel that the crocodiles are in the way.

Such concerns have encouraged many officials to take action. In southern Africa, for instance, lawmakers in Botswana have developed a unique protection program to address these problems. Throughout the country, whether on a sanctuary or on private land, all free-roaming wildlife is considered a natural resource, held in trust by the government. Crocodiles, therefore, are protected even if they swim down a river and stop on private land. For anyone to kill a crocodile legally, anywhere in the country, that person must have a hunting permit (which can cost fifteen hundred dollars or more). Additionally, Botswana is the first African nation to use computerized hunting licenses so that officials can keep track of what animals are killed and by whom, and they can immediately check, if questioned, to see whether someone has a valid permit.

Dealing with the public

Yet even with these laws in place, many local populations do not support protecting crocodile habitats or populations near their homes. This is because crocodiles do sometimes pose a physical threat to humans. In the Lower Shire Valley in Malawi, a country in southeast Africa, crocodiles kill an average of two Malawi-ans every day.

This poses a unique problem for conservationists, who know that in order to protect crocodiles local people must support the effort. According to Adam Britton,

What About the People?

Many of the world's developing nations also contain important natural resources, namely rain forests and mangrove swamps—the homes of crocodiles. Yet the human populations of these countries and their need for food and shelter place an exceptional demand on the environment. It is a situation that makes it difficult for those governments to protect dwindling crocodile populations. In his Spring 2000 article "Extinctions: Past and Present" for *Time,* Richard Leakey, a world-renowned paleontologist who has twice served as head of the Kenya Wildlife Service, addressed this concern.

> Can such countries justify setting aside national parks and nature reserves where human encroachment and even access is forbidden? Is it legitimate to spend large sums of money to save some species—be it an elephant or an orchid—in a nation in which a sizable percentage of the people are living below the poverty line?

Leakey's questions are echoed in debates between conservationists and human rights advocates, who have trouble justifying spending countless dollars on saving animal species when human lives are also at risk. It is an ongoing problem that organizations around the world are trying to solve. As yet, they have had little success.

> People who live around crocodilians need to see advantages in conserving them. It is difficult to see these people supporting conservation efforts if crocodilians have no intrinsic, aesthetic, environmental, economic, social or cultural value to them. . . . When animals threaten your livelihood, or even your life, it influences your opinion about those animals. Conservationists will have to bear this in mind if they hope to make long-term progress with conservation.[23]

One attempt to accomplish this is underway in Cuba. Every January the Cuban island of Isla de Juventud holds a crocodile festival, during which there are exhibits, displays, parades, student competitions, and many other events designed to involve the human community with their large reptile cohabitants. Along with the Cuban government, one of the sponsors of the festival is a local crocodile farm that

Adam Britton

Changing the negative perceptions about crocodiles has always been one of Adam Britton's goals. Britton is a zoologist with a lifelong passion for crocodilians. He travels extensively to study their biology, ecology, and population management. With a doctorate degree in zoology, he moved from his homeland of England to Australia and currently works as a research scientist for Wildlife Management International in Darwin, Australia, an area located in the Western Territory of Queensland, and home to thousands of estuarine and freshwater crocodiles. Britton has uncovered extensive information about crocodile behavior, especially about their vocalization and physiology. Along with his research, Britton lectures, writes articles, and has developed one of the most comprehensive websites on the subject of crocodilians.

raises the critically endangered Cuban crocodile, a species that lives in the island's Lanier Swamp. Only a few wild crocodiles remain in the area, and conservationists want to implement a plan to reintroduce the species to Lanier Swamp. However, for the Cuban crocodile to survive, it is necessary that the local population realizes the importance of the project and be willing to work with researchers to prevent the problems that could arise during reintroduction. For instance, the Cuban crocodile must be kept separate from the American crocodile, another species found in the area, so hybridization will not take place. It is also crucial to restrict the common caiman (an alligator species) from Cuban crocodile areas of the swamp so that the caiman, which is much bigger, will not eat juvenile Cuban crocodiles. Information about these and other crucial concerns are made part of the festival.

Scientific research

Public support is also important for the continual study of crocodiles and the ecosystems in which they live, two areas of interest many researchers believe will help protect crocodiles and their habitats. In fact, several institutions where such crocodile study occurs are also part of parks that are open to the public. The Guangdong Crocodile Research Institute in China is one. There, scientists learn about crocodiles through observation and detailed study. The captive crocodiles also make a great attraction for tourists. In the summers, thousands of crocodiles bask along the riverbanks, sleep in the shadows of trees, or swim in the river, enticing visitors to come to the facility and learn about the research being conducted there.

Another research facility is Wildlife Management International, located in Darwin, Australia. This facility houses Crocodylus Park, an educational area for the public. At Wildlife Management International, conservationists and scientists have been researching crocodiles for nearly thirty years, studying habits, determining what illnesses could threaten the animals, and learning more about what is necessary to improve crocodile reproduction. Most recently,

A baby American crocodile is weighed in Florida. Observing and studying crocodiles better enables researchers to help the animals survive.

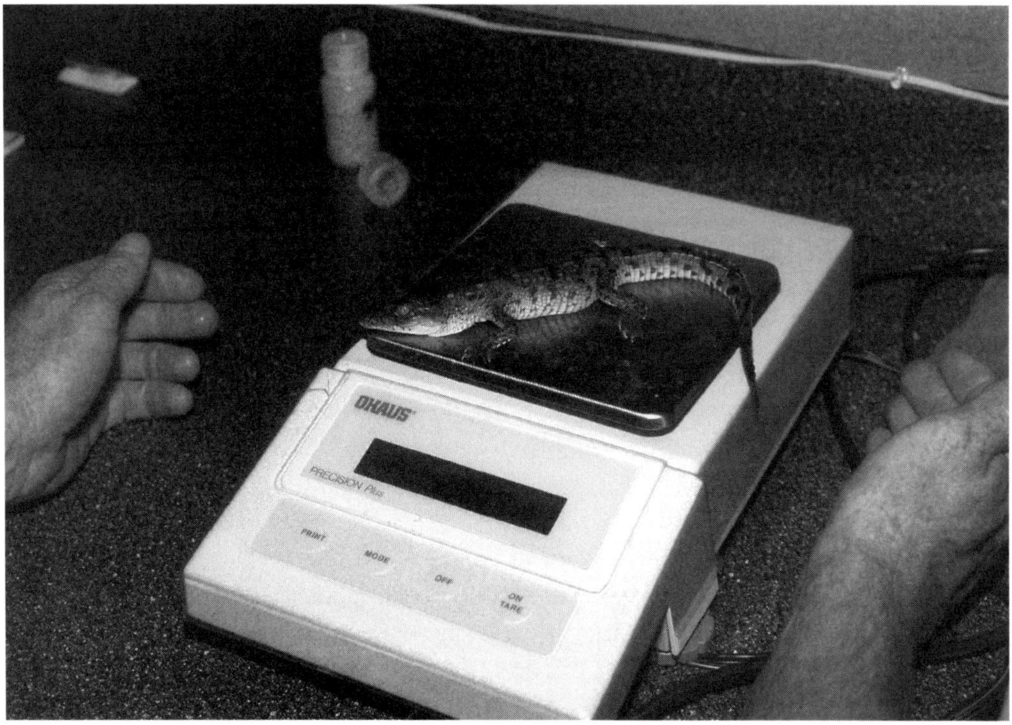

A Special Experience

Crocodile farms that are open to the public can have a positive effect on how people view crocodiles. Most farms have educated tour guides who provide information and answer questions about the animals. By walking beside the enclosed ponds and basking areas or visiting the hatching rooms, visitors can view the animals' behavior at close range.

Farm visitor Pat Costello clearly remembers a trip to one such facility. In an interview with the author, Costello describes his special experience.

> As part of a tour through the farm, the tourists were allowed to handle a crocodile egg that was near hatching time. I was at the end of the visitor line. The egg wiggled, and you could hear sounds from inside. It was obvious the baby was ready to get out. When the egg got to me, the farm guide began talking and everyone stopped to listen. After several moments, as I held the egg in my hand, the shell broke and the little crocodile forced its head through. It was something I'll never forget. It was incredible to be there at that point and have that little creature come out into the world right there in my hand. I interrupted the guide and told him what was happening. The baby squirmed out of the shell, and all of the tourists were allowed to hold it briefly before it was taken away. It made me more interested in crocodiles.

studies and research by Adam Britton have revealed a new protein in crocodile blood that may be a solution to antibiotic-resistant bacteria in humans. Britton's research continues and is just one more thing researchers hope will lead local populations to support this and other crocodile conservation projects.

International conservation organizations

Even with all of the parks, reserves, public support, and research facilities, protecting crocodiles—and endangered species in general—depends on national and international agreements. Most of these agreements have strong connections with the International Union for the Conservation of Nature (IUCN), the world's largest conservation-related organization. The three agreements of particular importance to crocodiles are the Convention on International Trade in Endangered Species of Wild Fauna and Flora (CITES) which is a treaty that regulates the trade and commerce of endangered species, the Ramsar Convention on Wetlands, and the World Heritage Committee.

The Ramsar Convention on Wetlands was developed in Ramsar, Iran, in 1971 as an international voluntary program. Today it has 123 member nations. Created to protect the world's wetlands, Ramsar is crucial to the maintenance of crocodile habitats because it offers aid to countries that want to develop conservation laws to protect wetlands.

Likewise, the World Heritage Committee, established a year later, created a list, called the World Heritage List, to catalog the areas it believes are in need of protection. The committee currently boasts more than 150 member countries and lists 690 properties. Although the properties are public land in their individual nations, the World Heritage Committee oversees their preservation. Of the 690 properties listed, 138 are natural or environmental sites, and of

To be successful, the protection of crocodiles must be an international effort.

those, more than one-third are ecosystems in which crocodiles live. The committee works to protect those sites, which includes the Sundarbans (a swamp in the Ganges Delta), the Serengeti, South Africa's Lake Saint Lucia, and the Florida Everglades.

Further aid to crocodile recovery has come from the Crocodile Specialist Group (CSG), a worldwide network of scientists and volunteers. This organization was developed not long after the CITES and Ramsar treaties were established, and it is also part of the IUCN. The CSG has established important documentation about individual crocodile species and factors that threaten the animals. They regularly visit crocodile habitats and take a census of the animals, estimate the reproduction rate, and examine nests and eggs for signs of abnormal development or disease. CSG experts also study crocodile habitats and note important changes that will effect the animals' natural behaviors.

A need to work together

The continued existence of many species of crocodiles depends on different countries around the world working together to uphold these international agreements, find resources to improve habitats, and come up with new ways to restock dwindling populations. Most governments, con-

A researcher collects eggs from a crocodile nest in India. The eggs will be examined for abnormal development and disease.

Researchers and conservationists from around the world are working together to ensure that crocodiles endure.

servationists, and researchers recognize this and do their best to support such cooperation. One example of this concerted effort occurred in March 1999, when the National Zoological Park in Washington, D.C., received two Philippine crocodiles from the Gladys Porter Zoo in Brownsville, Texas. Although the five-year-old crocodiles were hatched in the Texas zoo and were raised by Crocodile Conservation Services, a national organization, they actually belong to the government of the Philippines, a country where the species is critically endangered.

Another example of cooperation is an international meeting held by the IUCN every two years in a different country. Any interested herpetologists and environmentalists are invited to attend and discuss conservation issues that affect all crocodilians. The participants also hear reports from various researchers about specific species problems. In January 2000 the meeting was held in Cuba. One purpose of the meeting was to establish a rescue fund for the nearly extinct Chinese alligator and to generate additional support for the critically endangered Philippine and Siamese crocodiles.

Looking to the future

The improved conservation efforts and worldwide networks of herpetologists and environmentalists have had a dramatic and positive impact on the world's crocodile populations. Today, of fourteen crocodile species, only four remain critically endangered, with another two considered to be endangered. This recovery is quite an accomplishment. In a review of the effectiveness of crocodile conservation, the CSG reports,

> Bringing alligators, caimans, crocodiles, and gharials [or-gavials, long-snouted Indian crocodiles] back from the edge of extinction and returning them to former abundance is one of the true success stories in international wildlife conservation. . . . In only 25 years, 16 of the 23 species have been returned to abundance. This level of conservation success has not been achieved with primates, not with whales, not with spotted cats, not with parrots and macaws, nor with any other major group of wildlife.[24]

Researchers and conservationists hope that the various programs and increased public awareness will ensure that crocodiles survive another 100 million years.

Notes

Chapter 1: The Specialized Reptile

1. James Perran Ross, "Outlasting the Dinosaurs," *NOVA*. www.pbs.org/wbgh/nova/crocs.

Chapter 2: Crocodile Hunting

2. Adam Britton, "Monster Crocs." www.pbs.org/edens/kakadu/crocs.html.

3. Andrew Eriksen, "South Africa," *Crocodile Specialist Group Newsletter*, April–June 1999. www.flmnh.ufl.edu/natsci/herpetology/newsletter/news182b.htm#Africa.

4. James Perran Ross, ed., *Crocodiles: Status Survey and Conservation Action Plan*, 2nd ed., 1998. www.flmnh.ufl.edu/natsci/herpetology/act-plan/plan1998b.htm#Threats.

5. P. S. Soorae, "Lake Stephanie Crocodiles," *Crocodile Specialist Group Newsletter*, October–December 1997. www.flmnh.ufl.edu/natsci/herpetology/newsletter/news164a.htm#Africa.

6. Juan R. Bolanos, "Crocodile Situation Deteriorates in Tarcoles River," *Crocodile Specialist Group Newsletter*, January–March 1999. www.flmnh.ufl.edu/natsci/herpetology/newsletter/news181b.htm#CostaRica.

7. Quoted in Scott Fraser, "Zambia to Kill Man-Eating Crocodiles," *Crocodile Specialist Group Newsletter*, January–March 1998. www.flmnh.ufl.edu/natsci/herpetology/newsletter/news171b.htm#Zambia.

Chapter 3: Habitat Loss

8. Eugene Linden, "Condition Critical," *Time*, Spring 2000, p. 19.

9. Wetlands International, "Wetland Destruction." http://ngo.asiapac.net/wetlands/dest.htm.

10. John Thorbjarnarson, Steven G. Platt, and Saw Tun Khaing, "Ecological Reconnaissance of Meinmahla Kyun Wildlife Sanctuary and Vicinity, Southern Ayeyarwady Delta," *Crocodile Specialist Group Newsletter,* July–September 1999. www.flmnh.ufl.edu/natsci/herpetology/newsletter/news183b.htm#Myanmar.

11. Karen Free, "Land Issues Demand Tough Choices," *Habitat World,* August/September 2000, p. 11.

12. Ross, *Crocodiles.*

13. Solon L. Barraclough and Andréa Finger-Stich, "Some Ecological and Social Implications of Commercial Shrimp Farming in Asia," 1996. www.unrisd.org/engindex/pub/list/dp/dp74/shenv.htm.

Chapter 4: Crocodile Recovery

14. Quoted in Ross, *Crocodiles.*

15. Tim McGirk, "Crocodile City," *Times South Pacific,* August 31, 1998. www.britannica.com/bcom/magazine/article/0,5744,52025,00.html.

16. J. Hutton, "Reported from Ethiopa," *Crocodile Specialist Group Newsletter,* January–March 1998. www.flmnh.ufl.edu/natsci/herpetology/newsletter/news171b.htm#Ethiopia.

17. Britton, "Monster Crocs."

18. Steve Irwin, "Steve's Millennium 2000 Resolution." www.crocodilehunter.com/crocodile_hunter/about_steve_terri/steve_say.htm.

19. William E. Magnusson, "Where Is CSG Going?" *Crocodile Specialist Group Newsletter,* July–September 1994. www.flmnh.ufl.edu/natsci/herpetology/newsletter/news133a.htm#GUEST_EDITORIAL.

Chapter 5: Protecting Wild Populations and Habitats

20. Edward O. Wilson, "Vanishing Before Our Eyes," *Time,* Spring 2000, p. 30.

21. Thorbjarnarson, Platt, and Khaing, "Ecological Reconnaissance of Meinmahla Kyun Wildlife Sanctuary and Vicinity, Southern Ayeyarwady Delta."

22. Quoted in Mary Emanoil, ed., *Encyclopedia of Endangered Species.* Detroit: Gale Research, 1994, p. xvi.

23. Adam Britton, "A Brief History of Crocodilian Conservation." http://animals.discovery.com/features/crocodiles/conservation.htm.

24. Crocodile Specialist Group homepage. www.flmnh.ufl.edu/natsci/herpetology/crocs.htm.

Glossary

archipelago: A group of islands.

biodiversity: This word is a combination of the term *biological diversity* and refers to the variety of plants and animals found on the earth.

brackish: Somewhat salty.

carnivore: A species that consumes only the flesh of animals.

carrion: The dead and putrid flesh of any animal.

croakers: A name used to refer to newly hatching crocodiles, based on the sounds they make.

crustaceans: A class of aquatic animals such as crabs, lobsters, and shrimps.

deforestation: The act of removing large numbers of trees from forest areas.

ecosystem: A community of plants and animals that interact and function as an ecological unit.

embryo: A vertebrate at any stage of development before it is born or hatches.

estivation: To pass time in dormancy during drought seasons.

estuaries: Regions where rivers flow into oceans.

exploitation: To unjustly use something for one's own advantage.

fauna: Animal life typical of a special region or environment.

flora: Plant and bacterial life typical of a special region or environment.

gizzard: A secondary digestive area near the stomach, found especially in birds, that has thick muscular walls and a tough, horny lining for grinding food.

habitats: The homes of plants and animals, providing

everything they need to survive.

herpetology: A branch of zoology that deals with reptiles and amphibians.

impact: The significant effect of one event on another.

incubate: To maintain warmth and conditions favorable for hatching.

keystone: The chief element on which associated things depend for support.

monofilament: A single, untwisted strand of strong synthetic material such as nylon.

morphology: The form and structure of an organism or any of its parts.

mortality: The death of large numbers of animals in proportion to their population.

palate: The roof of the mouth, which separates the mouth from the nasal cavity.

poaching: To take game or fish in an unlawful manner.

poikilothermic: The scientific term for "cold blooded"—when an animal's body temperature is dependent on the temperature of its environment.

port of entry: A place where goods for trade are cleared through a customhouse to be certain they meet certain regulations.

safari: An extended hunting trip, usually in Africa, involving difficulty and danger.

sewage: Disposed refuse from house drains and streets.

species: A category of biological classification in which the related animals are capable of interbreeding.

temperate: Having a moderate climate.

treaty: A written contract between two or more political authorities that defines a specific arrangement.

vertebrates: Animals that possess a spinal column, including mammals, birds, reptiles, amphibians, and fish.

wetlands: Permanently or temporarily flooded regions where the soil's moisture content remains high.

Organizations to Contact

Crocodile Specialist Group (CSG)
Florida Museum of Natural History
P.O. Box 117800
Gainesville, FL 32611
website: www.flmnh.ufl.edu/natsci/herpetology/crocs.htm

This organization is part of the International Union for the Conservation of Nature's Species Survival Commission. The CSG brings together field research in herpetology and conservation in an attempt to reduce the threat to crocodile survival.

International Union for the Conservation of Nature (IUCN) Sustainable Use Initiative
1630 Connecticut Ave., 3rd Fl.
Washington, DC 20009
(202) 518-2053
website: www.iucn.org/themes/sui

The IUCN has many departments, offices, and commissions. This office focuses on the farming and ranching of crocodiles and other endangered species.

Ramsar Convention on Wetlands
Rue Mauverney 28
CH-1196 Gland, Switzerland
(011)41 22 999 0170
website: www.ramsar.org/index.html

This intergovernmental organization oversees the treaty agreements set up to preserve the world's wetlands.

Wildlife Conservation Society
185th St. and Southern Blvd.
Bronx, NY 10460-1099
website: www.wcs.org

The Wildlife Conservation Society integrates information from other agencies to monitor what is happening in certain habitats, such as the rain forests, and the species that live there.

Wildlife Management International
Crocodylus Park
815 McMillans Rd. Knuckey Lagoon
Darwin, Australia
website: http://wmi.com.au/index.html

Crocodylus Park is one of the first educational crocodile parks. With a staff of noted scientists, the research done here aids crocodiles throughout the world.

World Conservation Monitoring Centre (WCMC)
219 Huntingdon Rd.
Cambridge, CB3 0DL, UK
(011) 44 (0) 1223 277722
website: www.wcmc.org.uk

The WCMC is another organization that collects material from different sources to form an overview of what is happening to species and the environment.

Suggestions for Further Reading

Books

Harold Cogger and Richard Zweifel, eds., *Reptiles and Amphibians*. New York: Smithmark, 1992. This book presents information about reptiles and amphibians from prehistory to the present.

Daniel Cohen, *The Modern Ark: Saving Endangered Species*. New York: G. P. Putnam and Sons, 1995. This book tells of the efforts made by world zoos to maintain animals that are threatened in the wild.

Steve Grenard, *Handbook of Alligators and Crocodiles*. Melbourne, FL: Krieger, 1991. A good source of facts on specific crocodilians.

David Lambert, *The Field Guide to Prehistoric Life*. New York: Facts On File, 1985. This book provides good information about prehistoric times.

David White, *Deinosuchus*. Vero Beach, FL: Rourke Enterprises, 1989. An informative look at the first true crocodile.

Video

Discovery Channel, *The Ultimate Guide: Crocodiles*, March 1999. An informative video about crocodiles and their environments.

Websites

American Museum of Natural History (www.amnh.org/exhibition/expedition/endangered/croc/croc.html). This site has good general information about crocodiles.

Hartley's Creek Farm (www.hartleyscreek.com/). Here is information about crocodiles, and how crocodile farms work.

University of Michigan (http://animaldiversity.ummz.umich.edu/chordata/reptilia/crocodilia.html). This site gives detailed information about how crocodiles live.

World Heritage Convention (www.unesco.org/whc/index.htm). This website provides information from a key organization that attempts to preserve environmental and cultural sites around the world.

Works Consulted

Books

Raymond Bonner, *At the Hand of Man: Peril and Hope for Africa's Wildlife*. New York: Alfred A. Knopf, 1993. This book provides good information about the general state of the environment and conservation programs in Africa.

Mary Emanoil, ed., *Encyclopedia of Endangered Species*. Detroit: Gale Research, 1994. This encyclopedia offers specific information on all crocodilians as well as other endangered species.

Grahame J. W. Webb, S. Charlie Manolis, and Peter J. Whitehead, eds., *Wildlife Management: Crocodiles and Alligators*. Chipping Norton, NSW, Australia: Surrey Beatty & Sons, 1987. Contains conservation information about all crocodilians, with emphasis on those of Australia.

Edward O. Wilson, *The Diversity of Life*. Cambridge, MA: Harvard University Press, 1992. An academic treatise on biodiversity.

Periodicals

Associated Press, "Brazil Oil Spill," *USA Today*, January 22, 2000.

Wolfgang Bohme, "Remnant Crocs in the Sahara," *Science*, February 18, 2000.

Karen Free, "Land Issues Demand Tough Choices," *Habitat World*, August/September 2000.

Richard Leakey, "Extinctions: Past and Present," *Time*, Spring 2000.

Eugene Linden, "Condition Critical," *Time*, Spring 2000.

Paul Raeburn, "Save the Species—but Add Incentives," *Business Week*, January 18, 1999.

Tuxill and C. Bright, "Sharing the Planet: Can Humans and Nature Coexist?" *USA Today*, January 1999.

Edward O. Wilson, "Vanishing Before Our Eyes," *Time*, Spring 2000.

World Press Review, "Preserving Earth's Dwindling Species," October 1999.

Internet Sources

American Museum of Natural History. www.amnh.org/exhibitions/endangered/croc/croc.html.

Solon L. Barraclough and Andréa Finger-Stich, "Some Ecological and Social Implications of Commercial Shrimp Farming in Asia," 1996. www.unrisd.org/engindex/pub/list/dp/dp74/shenv.htm.

Juan R. Bolanos, "Crocodile Situation Deteriorates in Tarcoles River," *Crocodile Specialist Group Newsletter*, January–March, 1999. www.flmnh.ufl.edu/natsci/herpetology/newsletter/news181b.htm#CostaRica.

Adam Britton, "A Brief History of Crocodilian Conservation." http://animals.discovery.com/features/crocodiles/conservation.htm.

———, "Monster Crocs." www.pbs.org/edens/kakadu/crocs.html.

Crocodile Specialist Group homepage. www.flmnh.ufl.edu/natsci/herpetology/crocs.htm.

Crocodile Specialist Newsletter, "Crocodile Chairs," April–July 1999. www.flmnh.ufl.edu/natsci/herpetology/newsletter/news182b.htm#USA.

———, "Woman, 70, Killed by Crocodile in Jamaica," July–September 1999. www.flmnh.ufl.edu/natsci/herpetology/newsletter/news183b.htm#Jamaica.

Jennifer Daltry, "Siamese Crocodiles Discovered in the Cardamom Mountains," *Crocodile Specialist Group Newsletter,* April–June 2000. www.flmnh.ufl.edu/natsci/herpetology/NEWSLETTER/news192p7-12.htm#Cambodia.

Andrew Eriksen, "South Africa," *Crocodile Specialist Group Newsletter,* April–June 1999. www.flmnh.ufl.edu/natsci/herpetology/newsletter/news182b.htm#Africa.

Scott Fraser, "Zambia to Kill Man-Eating Crocodiles," *Crocodile Specialist Group Newsletter,* January–March 1998. www.flmnh.ufl.edu/natsci/herpetology/newsletter/news171b.htm#Zambia.

Carrie Hampton, "Crocodile Dundee," *Out There,* July 1997. www.outthere.coza/july97/wild4jul.html.

J. Hutton, "Reported from Ethiopa," *Crocodile Specialist Group Newsletter,* January–March 1998. www.flmnh.ufl.edu/natsci/herpetology/newsletter/news171b.htm#Ethiopia.

Steve Irwin, "Steve's Millennium 2000 Resolution." www.crocodilehunter.com/crocodile_hunter/about_steve_terri/steve_say.htm.

Alejandro Larriera, "Inspection of Crocodile Management," *Crocodile Specialist Group Newsletter,* October–December 1997. www.flmnh.ufl.edu/natsci/herpetology/newsletter/news164a.htm#PERU.

Tim McGirk, "Crocodile City," *Times South Pacific,* August 31, 1998. www.britannica.com/bcom/magazine/article/0,5744,52025,00.html.

William E. Magnusson, "Where Is CSG Going?" *Crocodile Specialist Group Newsletter,* July–September 1994. www.flmnh.ufl.edu/natsci/herpetology/newsletter/news133a.htm#GUEST_EDITORIAL.

James Perran Ross, "Outlasting the Dinosaurs," *NOVA.* www.pbs.org/wbgh/nova/crocs.

———, ed., *Crocodiles: Status Survey and Conservation Action Plan,* 2nd ed., 1998. www.flmnh.ufl.edu/natsci/herpetology/act-plan/plan1998b.htm#Threats.

P. S. Soorae, "Lake Stephanie Crocodiles," *Crocodile Specialist Group Newsletter,* October–December 1997. www.flmnh.ufl.edu/natsci/herpetology/newsletter/news164a.htm#Africa.

John Thorbjarnarson, Steven G. Platt, and Saw Tun Khaing, "Ecological Reconnaissance of Meinmahla Kyun Wildlife Sanctuary and Vicinity, Southern Ayeyarwady Delta," *Crocodile Specialist Group Newsletter,* July–September 1999. www.flmnh.ufl.edu/natsci/herpetology/newsletter/news183b.htm#Myanmar.

Wetlands International, "Wetland Destruction." http://ngo.asiapac.net/wetlands/dest.htm.

Interviews

Author interview with crocodile farm visitor Pat Costello, Montana, July 2000.

Index

Picture Credits

Cover Photo: © Gerry Ellis/ENP Images
© AFP/Corbis, 60
© Mary Beth Angelo, The National Audubon Society Collection/Photo Researchers, 81
Associated Press AP, 77
© Dave Bartruff/Corbis, 15
© Jonathan Blair/Corbis, 21, 22, 23, 25, 26, 40, 59, 70
© Tom Brakefield/Corbis, 91
© W. Perry Conway/Corbis, 73, 87
© Digital Vision, Ltd., 46, 51
© David Fleetham, 1999/FPG International, 13
Fox Photos/Hulton Getty Collection/Archive Photos, 29
© Michael Freeman/Corbis, 90
© Gallo Images/Corbis, 37, 63
© Farrell Grehan, 1991/FPG International, 19
© Chinch Gryniewicz; Ecoscene/Corbis, 69
© C. A. W. Guggisberg, The National Audubon Society Collection/Photo Researchers, 14
Ernst Haas/Hulton Getty Collection/Archive Photos, 7
Hulton Getty Collection/Archive Photos, 30, 49
© Wolfgang Kaehler/Corbis, 80
© Catherine Karnow/Corbis, 83
© George Lepp/Corbis, 55
© Ludovic Maisant/Corbis, 78
© George McCarthy/Corbis, 89
© Tom McHugh, The National Audubon Society Collection/Photo Researchers, 38
© Douglas Peebles/Corbis, 53
© Peter Philipp; Viennaslide Photoagency/Corbis, 65
© Stan Osolinski, 1992/FPG International, 52
© Stan Osolinski, 1998/FPG International, 8, 56
© The Purcell Team/Corbis, 18
Reuters/Jason Reed/Archive Photos, 64
© Jeffrey L. Rotman/Corbis, 43
© Kevin Schafer/Corbis, 32
© Paul A. Souders/Corbis, 34
© Telegraph Colour Library/ FPG International, 11
© Jim Tuten, 1994/FPG International, 75
© ULF SJOSTEDT, 1996/FPG International, 67

About the Author

Karyn Follis Cheatham has been a research analyst, livestock photographer, math and history tutor, sports editor, print model, university adviser for Native American recruitment, and choir director. But she is first and always a writer. She has published six books, many articles and poetry, and has been an editor for textbooks and newsletters. For a number of years, her writing and photography appeared regularly in a national rodeo magazine. With her interests in outdoor activities, she has camped and traveled throughout the United States. When at home, she shares her time with a dog and two horses and is a volunteer tutor at an after-school facility.